THE SPIRITUAL LAWS OF CREATION

The Crucial Knowledge for Humankind

CHARLES S. BROWN

THE SPIRITUAL LAWS OF CREATION
The Crucial Knowledge for Humankind
Charles S. Brown

http://www.crystalbooks.org

This Edition published in New Zealand by
Crystal Publishing.
P.O. Box 60042, Titirangi,
West Auckland, New Zealand

First Edition 2005
Second Edition 2007
Final Edition 2012

Copyright © 2005 – 2007 – 2012 Charles S. Brown

All rights reserved. No part of this publication may be reproduced, stored in a retrieval system, or transmitted in any form, or by any means, electronic, mechanical, photocopying, recording or otherwise, without the prior permission of the publisher.

Moreover, this book is sold on the condition that it shall not, by way of trade or otherwise, be lent, re-sold, hired out or otherwise circulated without the publisher's prior consent in any form of binding or cover other than that in which it is published and without this condition being imposed on the subsequent purchaser.

ISBN 978-0-9582627-5-0

Contents

Acknowledgements		5
Preface		7
The Spiritual Laws: The Necessary Knowledge		11
0.1	The Nature of the Spiritual Principles.	22
0.2	The Law of Movement!	26
	0.2.1 Movement = Life.	26
0.3	The Law of Reciprocal Action!	30
	0.3.1 Decisions Produce Consequences.	30
	0.3.2 Faith Versus Works.	31
	0.3.3 Attitude to the Suffering.	46
	0.3.4 "Ten Men Will Take Counsel And It Will Come To Nought."	48
	0.3.5 The Interlinked Global Monetary System: Reaping the Whirlwind! 'A Brief History Lesson.'	56
0.4	The Law of Attraction of Similar Species!	73
	0.4.1 Like Attracts Like.	73
	0.4.2 Spiritual Qualities as the First Consideration.	78
	0.4.3 Families and Children.	79
	0.4.4 Why there is so much Violence and Evil on Earth. The "Divine Warning" to Mothers!	86
	0.4.5 The Universal Pain of Childbirth. The Enlarging Baby Cranium: A Medical "Mystery".	91

0.4.6 The Enlarging Baby Cranium:
The "Lawful" Reason! 98

0.4.7 Sexual Orientation and Creation-Law. 106

0.5 The Law of Spiritual Gravity! 114

0.5.1 Gravity! – The Spiritual Dynamic. 114

0.6 The Law of Balance! 117

0.6.1 Balance in Life! – A Vital Necessity. 117

0.6.2 To Give, or to Take? 125

0.7 The Law of Rebirth! 132

0.7.1 Rebirth! – Fact or Fiction? 132

0.8 Grace! – A Gift of Divine Love. 141

Conclusion **145**

0.8.1 A Brief Illustration of Why Recognition of
The Law is a "Crucial Imperative" for all of
humanity right now. 146

0.9 Postscript. 148

Bibliography. **149**

0.10 The Parent Book: 151

Acknowledgements.

The foundational format for this Booklet, derived from its Parent Work: – **BIBLE "MYSTERIES" EXPLAINED: Understanding "Global Societal Collapse" from The "Science" in The Bible; What Every Scientist, Bible Scholar and Ordinary Man Needs to Know**
– singularly acknowledges the work of Stephen Lampe, author of particular and vital Spiritual publications.
See Bibliography.

His kind permission to use essential material from those works has resulted in more complete and clarified explanations of **"The Spiritual Laws"** – **Creation-Law** – than might otherwise have been the case.

Preface.

The notion that Universal Laws or Laws of Life govern what takes place "out there" in the cosmos is probably an easily accepted idea for most. The constancy of the motion of the stars testify to the existence of a powerful force operating to hold star systems in relative stability. The great scientist and astronomer, Sir Isaac Newton noted that "only a few fundamental laws" governed the Universe. He also believed the same laws applied on earth. So the concept of Universal Law is a well-established idea in the psyche of humankind. Most religions, too, accept and teach that certain sacrosanct laws exist, and are necessary for societal stability and harmony.

Basic and fundamental "rules" such as are found in the three great monotheistic religions vis-à-vis, "The Ten Commandments" of the Christian faith, for example, can be clearly seen as inherently possessing the highest standards for living spiritually-correctly. Most religions and spiritual teachings similarly possess such guidelines. The further out we extend this theme, however, the more contentious the whole paradigm becomes. When we examine The Laws of different cultures and ethnic groups we find ideas that differ markedly from the standard accepted by the great religions of the world – not that those followers necessarily practise what they ostensibly believe. Thus huge differences reveal themselves in human interpretations of this enigmatic concept called "The Law".

In terms of the Christian Faith, it is probably fair to say that many Christians would believe that the Ten Commandments *are*

The Law. The Book of Leviticus also offers specific detail of precise law covering all aspects of human relationships. Often thought to relate to Jewish life, culture and religion solely, The Laws outlined in Leviticus reveal specific "spiritual aspects" that are relevant for *all* peoples, simply by virtue of the fact that we all possess, and are affected by, precise natural processes centred on the human body. Whilst these aspects of Law are clearly that, is this The Law that Jesus referred to as that which He came "not to overthrow"? Or is there more?

The Spiritual Laws of which we speak can be stated to be that force or power which drives to its relevant, appropriate and commensurate end, a justified outworking resulting from the decisions we make. Whether made as individuals or globally-collectively, The Spiritual Laws return to us the consequences deriving from those decisions. In concert with that reality, the many parables of Jesus exactly illustrate the operation of The Spiritual Laws of Creation in the affairs of men. The outworking of the power inherent in them also brought into being the actual Creations, and the same power sustains and maintains it all. It is thus the primary factor in ensuring that we have an earthly home in which to exercise our free-will attribute, and thereby receive our appropriate "return/s".

The key Law in this case is called: "The Law of Reciprocal Action". We know it more generally in its religious guise as: "What a man sows, that shall he reap." Science broadly notates the same process as: "For every action there is an equal and opposite reaction." Relatively few in number, these very exacting Laws, by virtue of their unchangeable and thus inviolable nature, precisely determine and dispense appropriate and perfect justice specifically commensurate with the kind of transgression made.

Completely automatic in operation, The Spiritual Laws take no account of religious, cultural, scientific or even political determinations and proclamations. Neither do they take into account whether or not humankind is even aware of them. **They simply are**. Only with the knowledge of them, and thus how they work in their individual and collective outworking, can earthly humanity ever hope to understand not just *why* the world is in crisis, but why concerted international efforts by so many well-meaning groups are not able, for the long term, to effect fundamental and sweeping change for the better. Thus, global societies continue to rapidly unravel despite such efforts.

Since The Spiritual Laws provide the only sure mechanism where-by positive change can be wrought across the globe, rapid adjustment to them is imperative. However, given the diverse and fractious divisions permeating world societies, such a vision is simply not possible. That being the case in the collective sense, we can at least *individually* awaken to the recognition of them and thereby gift to ourselves the exact mechanism whereby we can attain peace of mind at this time of frightening and uncertain change.

The Spiritual Laws! The Crucial Knowledge.

Oh the Ancient Truth!
Ages upon ages past it was found,
And it bound together a Noble Brotherhood.
The Ancient Truth!
Hold fast to it!

(Goethe. Italics mine.)

Without Revelation a Nation fades.
But it prospers **by knowing the Law***!*

(Proverbs. Chapter 29: Verse 18)

"I come not to overthrow the Law but to fulfil it!"

(Matthew. 5:17-18)

Three different quotes, but all relevant to the notion we inherently possess that "law" is both necessary and desirable for any society to function well. But what was or is this Law that Jesus as The Son of God stated He had come "not to overthrow", but "to fulfil"? If He came to fulfil The Law, and not to overthrow it, it must surely mean that that Law of which He spoke could not be overthrown, not even by Him as The Son (or Part) of God. That would further translate to the clear fact that just as He had to obey that Law so, too, are we all necessarily subject in the same way to the same Law. More than the "Law of Moses" – and not that interpreted by the religious authorities of the day in sterile rigidity – but that same Law given *spiritual life and significantly added to* in Divine Power and greater Knowledge!

This Booklet examines certain and precise Laws which govern all life and to which all human decisions and processes are subject. In their inherent Perfection these Laws are thus Absolute and therefore Inviolable and Unchangeable in their perfect outworking. The understanding of The Spiritual Laws is imperative for the complete understanding of the aim and purpose of this essay. And that is **to know The Law**. As stated above:

"*Without Revelation a Nation fades.* **But it prospers by knowing The Law!**"

Only by virtue of that crucial knowledge might we thus know why the mainly dark and bloodthirsty actions of humankind over millennia **must** call forth a Judgement upon itself. It is a judgement, however, perfectly **just** in its application, for it will be exactly commensurate with the degree of good or evil that the various groups and races within humanity have visited upon each other over that period of time. The reader should therefore strive to understand the explanations that *interlink* the different Laws.

In the context of religious thinking and cultural tradition the word "spiritual" may mean any number of things. In its distilled essence and form, however, *it should mean only one thing.* By **Spiritual**, we should mean "of the spirit" i.e., that which is **not** of the material but which occupies the *higher level*. We should not use this word to describe things that are concerned solely with the mundane and earthly, including some aspects of traditional cultures. And we certainly should not debase the inherent noble power of the word by attempting to ascribe to it practices or beliefs such as those pertaining to occult or psychic activity, for example.

If we, however, describe this word as being more uplifting, more noble in its origin, and therefore in its application more able to offer those higher virtues capable of producing the best kind of society; and if it *is* that which originates from out of the Highest Spheres, are we not then talking of absolutes? Are we speaking, then, of possibly needing to apply "rules" to achieve that desired state? And are we, in the final analysis, stating that such a thing can only be possible under clear, uniform, strict and **unchangeable Laws**!

Our answer to all of the above is an unequivocal yes! We can, moreover, state such "guidelines" to be that perfection which is naturally inherent within **The Spiritual Laws**. It is thus important to clarify this amorphous thing called "The Law" in order to give better understanding of some of the many *incorrect* interpretations of this vitally important life-word – **"Spiritual"**. And therewith strive to illustrate its true meaning, thereby separating the beneficial from the clearly unhelpful, and certainly from the dangerous.

Irrespective of the basic tenets of the many and varied religions on earth, The Law is invariably *perceived to have*, as its underlying foundation, a higher being or beings who are the guardians of that "Law", with those same beings watching over the people to whom they will have given it! Throughout history many races have striven to base their societies upon the ideal of The Law, with the Jewish people perhaps possessing the strongest application of it in their long history. If one reads the Old Testament as an historical document rather than as a religious one, it is very clear that the ancient Israelites *only* prospered when they *obeyed* The Law. When they rejected it outright or even simply adopted the laws of the peoples around them, they invariably suffered invasion, enslavement and, at times, terrible slaughter.

By definition, the *customary law* of any race of people can *only* derive from the beliefs, customs and traditions that that particular group will have believed was correct for them at a particular time in their development. Unfortunately, however, the historical record for many ethnic groups and tribal societies reveal their particular law/lore as being also strongly derived from their *fears and superstitions*. So whilst that "customary law" may have served well for a given time of development, if a race proceeds normally and naturally through the various stages of "spiritual" growth and development, certain factors of that law should clearly change as greater insights hopefully lead away from the fear and/or superstitious aspects perhaps previously present within that group.

The nature of The Spiritual Laws or Principles therefore decree that they are the only model on which to base any society today because, ***by their very constitution***, they are absolutely inviolable and unchangeable. Since these absolute parameters logically further decree that such Laws unequivocally transcend humankind's generally narrow views; in their clear perfection they are thus the ideal foundation for all societies and ethnic groups. Whilst we should certainly examine all laws which contribute to the sum total of all legislation that a given country or people might possess, only those aspects which accord with The Spiritual Laws should be retained. That which does not do so should be discarded once more correct laws are formulated to replace them.

This Booklet explains those crucial Laws!

The English empiricist philosopher, John Locke, (1632-1704) notable for his "Two Treatises of Government" which justified the English Revolution of 1688 opposing the notion of the "divine right of Kings", held the view that the idea of God was a "potential" of human reason. And that it was likely for human reason to know that God exists. Most of the Enlightenment philosophers also believed in the "reality" of a God, for the world was far too rational for that not to be the case, in their general view.

At times of human suffering, and given this seemingly inherent belief in God on the part of humankind, it is therefore not surprising to hear the anguished cries of; "If there is a God of Love, how can He let this happen?"; "How can there be a God of Love when there is so much misery and suffering in the world?'; "How can it be?", "Why him, her, them?"; "Why did they have to be taken?"; "I don't understand it!" etc., etc..

Very great puzzlement is also evinced at the seemingly unfair and untimely death of "good" people or young children, or in the birth of the handicapped. Yet whilst there may not generally be clear understanding of the reasons for such seemingly "hard fate", the very fact that many people ask why "God should allow it" appears to bear out the Enlightenment philosophers belief of a probable knowing within man of the existence of a great and **All-Mighty "Creator"**.

Therein lies our conundrum, our non-understanding! We feel great pain and anguish during times of deep sorrow because the ultimate reason *why* is often difficult to understand. Words of solace and condolence are offered but, whilst they are comforting, they may not provide answers. What is then left? An experience that *can* serve to bring people together, but also an event – if deeply traumatic – with the potential to shatter lives and split families apart. And, moreover, can unfortunately also reduce the quality of life of those affected because the nature of the event itself and the ongoing memory of it may not *appear* to offer any logical reasons as to why. The resultant legacy may well be the inability to ever find reasons or answers, thus resulting in ongoing and unresolved heartache. Yet to be faced with seemingly unfair "blows of fate" should act as the *strongest* impetus to ask the key question – **why**?

The Enlightenment philosophers encouraged rational enquiry about God by rejecting any mysterious doctrines and maintaining that the existence of God could be arrived at by introspection and human experience. However, it would be unhelpful if we became so absorbed in our enquiry or search that much else that is worthwhile and valuable in life is excluded. Therefore, in the continuation of one's life, one should adjust one's thinking and perhaps one's lifestyle to support the aim of finding that reason why. In order to find such answers, however, there must logically be some rational mechanism whereby this can be achieved.

The premise postulated here is that only with the knowledge of The Spiritual Laws of Creation can sense ever be made of our existence and our reason for being. Only a thorough knowledge of The Spiritual Laws can provide a logical "thought-process mechanism" through which the question of apparently unfair and/or "hard blows of fate" can be answered. And thereby offer the potential for a more benign and enlightened global society than is currently the case. A brief introduction to just two points of "The Law" should suffice to illustrate why there is such an entrenched general refusal by humankind to acknowledge the existence of Spiritual Law – let alone the inviolability of it. The same two points will further demonstrate how beliefs that do not acknowledge The Spiritual Laws effectively prevent basic understanding of the why of life's tragedies anyway.

Firstly, it is probably reasonable to assume that most people accept the notion that we possess "free will" i.e., we can, and do, make decisions for ourselves virtually every minute of each day. Also, personal decisions via this mechanism should allow us full command over our individual destinies. If this were not so, we would be forced to assume that what happens in our lives is determined by factors outside our control. If such an "arbitrary force" did actually exist, it might perhaps have to be regarded as a mischievous or even rogue one given that some people seem to suffer more setbacks than might reasonably be expected to occur in a 'normal' life.

Secondly, the simple act of making a decision about anything must presuppose an outcome of some kind. Most students of religion, philosophy, or even homespun logic will probably accept the concept that "what one sows one must, or shall, reap". Certainly for the general Christian community, this Biblical directive is sacrosanct in its perceived truth. If that is so, there must logically be a just and lawful mechanism that produces the outcome or the reaction to every decision made. Now, if it is reasonable to assume the first part of the equation – that there will be an outcome from a decision made – then it is surely equally reasonable to assume the second; that there **will be a return** – without fail! The premise here is that ultimately it is our own decisions which therefore determine all outcomes that affect us.[1]

What happens, however, when these two cornerstones, i.e., the notion of *free will* and, *we reap what we sow*, are brought together to try to make sense of tragedy and misfortune? For if each notion is true, and this work unequivocally accepts that truth, then any misfortune – and it is usually only misfortunes and tragedies that produce any kind of soul-searching for answers anyway – must have been set in place somewhere, sometime, **by the reaper**. Therefore, if we consider the heart of the two particular tenets to be absolute, then the **first absolute** would naturally presuppose that the **second one** is also – in terms of a logical and meaningful **connection and outcome**.

However, because the *reasons* for misfortunes are not always *immediately* apparent – whereby the concept and logic of "free will" and its equally logical *connection* of "reaping the effects" is clearly *visible* and thus understandable – it becomes necessary to attempt to postulate some kind of *different* mechanism as an explanation, or to despair of ever knowing why. The clear contention stated in *this* particular equation is that if both tenets are absolute and sacrosanct as an inviolable Law, then we cannot possibly postulate other reasons which exclude or alter either one to simply fabricate any such connection between our *free-will decision-making ability*, and *reaping what we sow*. And we certainly should not try to make it conveniently fit a religious doctrine or dogma or, indeed, any

---

[1] Science, in essence, states this process thus: "For every action there is an equal and opposite reaction."

personal faith/belief mode.

Whilst we therefore possess the inherent freedom to make any kind of decision we may wish to, we must clearly recognise that we are absolutely *not free* to choose to *either accept or reject* the returning consequences! Under the inviolability of this absolute *equation of life*, **consequences must always derive from decisions**! That is the clear and unequivocal reality.

Now, if the two tenets are *not* accepted as being absolute and thus lawfully connected, then searching outside these two sacrosanct positions to try to find an answer might perhaps *seemingly* provide "other" alternatives. However if such an *answer* **denies** the inherently logical and thus lawful connection between a "free-will decision" and "...reaping what one has sown" – i.e., accepting that there must naturally be a consequence from making a decision in the first place – then that particular position naturally refutes the inherent inviolability of any "lawful connection" to begin with. Yet the two inviolable "cornerstones" of this *equation of life* unequivocally state that they clearly *must be absolute*, both in essence and reality.

The inviolability of "inherent justice" naturally contained within The Spiritual Laws ensures that they will *always* provide correct answers. It is an infallible mechanism that not only does *not* compromise the absolute nature of the two "cornerstones" of our illustration but positively strengthens the interlinking of all The Spiritual Laws to provide genuine solutions! Therefore, since the two "cornerstones" *are* absolute and lawfully connected, the clear contention here is that another Law – equally as valid and sacrosanct – must be taken into account if one wishes to understand **all** connections. It is that *other* law, not generally recognised and accepted, which provides the key. Unfortunately, it is the refusal to accept this factual Law that gives rise to so much confusion and anguish when needing to find answers – for major problems, particularly.

That *'decisive Law'* – **The Law of Rebirth** – is fully explained further on.

The concept of reincarnation, whilst not generally accepted by most Western religions or the scientific community, is an absolute belief for hundreds of millions worldwide. Multi-earth lives provide the mechanism whereby the two "spiritually-lawful" cornerstones of *free will* and *reaping what one sows* can be logically explained. More particularly where an earth-life does not offer sufficient time for certain categories of "reaping" to occur. It is not for nothing that Jesus stated quite emphatically, "Seek, and You Shall Find"

(Matt. 7:7) He, by virtue of His Divine Origin, spoke always from the knowledge of The Spiritual Laws of Creation! He was able to survey all happenings, both the small and the large, in their complete cycles from cause to effect. Therefore, if any answers are to give a true and comprehensive explanation, ***they must first explain it*** spiritually.

In contrast to the spiritual point of view taught by Jesus, a purely medical, scientific, religious, political or sociological explanation for a particular problem can only take in the material effect. Though the end *effect* may be seen or felt in the material, it is, nevertheless, the *result* of a "spiritually-willed" decision made somewhere, sometime by someone individually, or some group collectively. By virtue of its purely material application, earthly disciplines are therefore not able to give a complete overview for they are not always able to see the actual starting point of such outcomes, irrespective of views to the contrary from within the individual disciplines. This is not to decry the very great help that we can obviously obtain from disciplines concerned with empirical paradigms. However, where it is a question of finding the actual source of many of our problems, or the answers to life itself, earth-orientated practices are not able to supply this. Because only in Spiritual Law and Its Source can we find these ultimate answers!

Despite the superiority of the Spiritual viewpoint over the materialistic one, the whole thrust of our much-vaunted, modern education system virtually denies the existence of anything other than what can be materially seen, heard, felt, or measured. Currently, the scientific and rationalist point of view reigns supreme. But there are other voices questioning the narrow strictures of such points of view. These voices are slowly swelling in volume and some are coming from within the scientific disciplines too. In essence, the realisation may be slowly dawning that all we have been taught to blindly accept through the education and religious systems may prove to be very different from the actual reality.

So, from where springs this irrational attitude and widespread denial that seeks to deny man the knowledge of his true Spiritual self, and therewith his actual origin? Should this not be the ultimate goal of the various disciplines rather than the present one of attempting to steer all away from this so-called "irrational and unscientific" view? Is there fear, then, of this unscientific, perhaps politically and even culturally incorrect word, – **SPIRITUAL?**

The obvious problem encountered when discussing **The Spiritual** is that the very word itself is generally lumped with whatever ideas humankind may determine it to encompass. Things that originate from, or are connected to, the actual Spiritual Realm, can be deemed to be genuinely Spiritual. And because *only* the *truly* spiritual can *actually* be of **The Spiritual**, what is of that Realm is therefore sacred.

However, because the Realm of the so-called "beyond" is generally deemed as being "all spiritual", anything that is connected with or derived from it is also viewed similarly by some religions and cultures. Far too much is made of purely man-made icons being designated sacred and therefore regarded as spiritual in humankind's estimation. Thus there exists the farcical idea that everything that man *decides* is sacred must therefore be so and, by extension, also spiritual and thus holy. **Nothing could be further from the truth.**

In fact some aspects of various cultures, such as the meanings ascribed to grotesque carved images or in particular ancient practices to name two examples, are so aspiritual in both form and connection that it is difficult to even begin to understand how their supporters ever arrived at such a conclusion. The Spiritual Laws of Creation offer clear, objective solutions as to how a more open and correct mind-set can free cultural emotionalism or scientific rigidity from self-imposed and inculcated beliefs that stubbornly cling to a wrong understanding of this vitally important *life-word* – **SPIRITUAL!**

The greatest teacher humankind has ever had is history, and within its pages may be found the struggle of individuals who have been lone and lonely "voices in the wilderness". Boat-rockers they were, all of them, with voices that were raised in protest against blindness and, at times, sheer stupidity. Voices of people who possessed the clarity of vision or perception to *know* that certain "official" teachings and views were gravely in error. Those same lone courageous voices were often stilled, silenced, to protect the ego and power base of those in authority who fought to maintain, *at all costs,* the "official version".

In some cases the lone voices were able to convince the "authorities" of the correctness of their beliefs, though often after years of protest. Then, in an absolute farce, the "new knowledge" became the accepted norm. A norm or standard not only *accepted* by the ruling authority, but also *promoted* by it as being correct and therefore suitable for the masses. Do we think that it is any different today? No we do not. For mankind's collective ego has not yet humbled itself sufficiently to *voluntarily* recognise the very truth of what we assert here; that historically, the essence of truth has never lain with the masses – only with the few!

A classic example is that of the view of Ptolemy (*ca.* AD 90-168), a Graeco-Egyptian mathematician and geographer who believed that the earth was the centre of the universe and that the sun and planets revolved around it. In stating this view, he set in place a theory that remained unchallenged for about 1600 years. The main reason for such a long acceptance of a wrong belief was that it perfectly suited the egocentric interpretation of the church. And no voice was raised against it until 1543 when Copernicus, (1473 -1543) a Polish astronomer, found that only with the sun at the centre of the universe could the planetary system work. From that point on the Ptolemaic belief was rejected – at least by the newly emerging sciences.

Unfortunately, this was not a belief shared by the Church and is graphically illustrated in the persecution of Galileo (1564-1642) by the Inquisition in 1633. Galileo, an Italian astronomer and mathematician, agreed with the claim of Copernicus that the sun was the centre of our universe. This "unacceptable view", however, led to his persecution. He recanted, but is said to have muttered under his breath: "But it [the Earth] does move."[2]

Another stark example was the debate between flat-earth theorists, led by the European Church, and the opposite belief that the earth was spherical; accepted by scholars in some monasteries. Accepted also by Columbus and other navigators as being the *probable* truth, the latter purely by their logical observations of the curved and disappearing horizon. History records that the journey of Columbus forced an immediate change of view within "the establishment". Long before then, however, Greek mathematicians already understood the truth of a spherical earth.

What the teaching "authorities" should learn to accept is that the very nature of truth guarantees that it cannot be stifled or suppressed forever. It would be far better for them to keep a completely open mind to *"all voices"*. The one constant that will determine the *validity* of any definition of "the Spiritual" will be whether or not it accords with the actual Spiritual Laws themselves, thereby separating the "superficial voices" from the "true ones". The lawful mechanism contained within the Living Law thus determines

---

[2] It is interesting to note that Copernicus did not publish his theory until the year of his death at age 70. Perhaps it was a purposeful decision on his part to publish as late as was possible for him in an effort to escape the censure of the Church.

which "voices" will ultimately fail, and which will stand the test of time. This is the only true measure as these Laws are, themselves, eternal. And within the life-path parameters given for humankind it is we who must finally acknowledge and accept this fact, since our life, being and sustenance are given only via these Laws.

To glibly state that mankind is "not meant to understand the ways of The Creator" presupposes the requirement to submit to and accept all suffering in fatalistic ignorance. The Spiritual Laws decree that we actually **are** "masters of our own destiny", even if present events seem to suggest otherwise. It is our refusal to accept the Truth of the Law, *as it actually is,* that is the problem. The above historic examples together with the previously postulated premise that we are masters of our own destiny indicate that no one should be afraid to abandon dogma when it becomes apparent that it is clearly not true. We should especially beware of leaders who knowingly still maintain the old errors out of fear of a collapse of their authority and organisation.

On the relationship between science and religion, the scientific giant Albert Einstein observed:

> "Intelligence makes clear to us the interrelation of means and ends. But mere thinking cannot give us a sense of the ultimate and fundamental ends. To make clear these fundamental ends and valuations, and to set them fast in the emotional life of the individual, seems to me precisely the most important function which religion has to perform in the social life of man. And if one asks whence derives the authority of such fundamental ends, since they cannot be stated and justified merely by reason, one can only answer: they come into being *not through demonstration* **but through revelation**, *through the medium of powerful personalities*. One must not attempt to justify them, but rather to sense their nature simply and clearly."
>
> (Albert Einstein, *Ideas and Opinions*, p 42-3. Bonanza Books, New York, Italics mine.)

We therefore state unequivocally that there should be no contradiction between science and religious truth, and that science cannot supersede any such truths. Though noting the demarcation between science and religion, Einstein also understood the strong reciprocal relationships and dependencies between the two. He stated:

> "Though religion may be that which determines the goal, it has, nevertheless learned from science, in the broadest sense, what means will contribute to the attainment of the goals it has set up. *But science can only be created by those who are thoroughly imbued with the aspiration toward truth and understanding.*"

Einstein summarises his view of the relationship between science and religion thus: *"Science without religion is lame, religion without science is blind."* — (Italics mine.)

0.1 The Nature of the Spiritual Principles.

> "The Laws of Creation derive their eternal validity from the fact of God's Perfection. On account of God's Perfection, His Will is therefore perfect. Consequently, The Laws manifesting This Will are also necessarily perfect. They cannot be improved upon, and they remain absolutely unchangeable."
>
> (Building Future Societies The Spiritual Principles, p 23. Stephen Lampe, Millennium Press.)

This inviolable premise logically stipulates that God cannot act in an arbitrary manner and "do anything He wants". It may certainly be convenient to offer this sort of explanation to a difficult religious question thereby seeming to temporarily get rid of the problem, but it still, nonetheless, awaits a correct answer.

For if God is able to do "anything He wants" by virtue of the fact that He Is God, **where then lies His Perfection**? Since it **must** logically follow that if He Is Perfect and His Laws are Perfect and therefore unchangeable, then any belief that states otherwise *automatically* casts doubt on this accepted belief in **"A Perfect God"**. Quite simply, any attempt to change a *Perfect Law* naturally implies that the Law could not have been perfect in the first instance – if it then needed to be changed.

It is thus impossible to impute imperfection to a Perfect God!

Therefore the recognition of The Laws of Creation, *as they actually are in their inviolability*, will finally return to God the Perfection that Is His.

Two thousand years ago Jesus, arguably the greatest, most wonderful "boat rocker" of all, gave stern warning to the, then, leaders of the Church. The fact that He did not support their practices is clearly apparent by virtue of His condemnation of them. The same lawful condemnation applies today to all teachings and disciplines that attempt to suppress the Truth.

> "Woe to you, play-acting professors and Pharisees! because you lock up the Kingdom of Heaven in the face of mankind; while you yourselves neither enter, nor allow those arriving to go in."
>
> (Matthew 23:13, Fenton.)

In accordance with that clear message, it is our conviction that there are certain Spiritual Laws or principles that guide and determine the course of everything throughout Creation, including the destiny of man on Earth. These Laws are Eternal i.e., they have existed from eternity. Everything in Creation, including humankind, came into being via the operation of these Laws, and our continued existence here depends on them also. The originator of these Laws is **"God, The Creator"**. Only what is inherent in His Laws of Creation can ever come to full flower and be sustained in Creation. By extension, all else i.e., activities not supported by those Laws, *must inevitably fail*.

Even though The Spiritual Laws allowed us the gift of conscious life, they have not always been clearly recognised. Throughout man's long and convoluted history, great and wise spiritual teachers arose at varying intervals to call attention to them, Teachers such as Krishna, Zoroaster, Lao-Tse, Moses and the Prophets, Buddha, Mohammed – and Jesus. At best, their Teachings were sometimes not understood or sometimes misinterpreted. At worst, they were *knowingly* distorted.

Because The Laws *were* insufficiently understood, misinterpreted, taken out of context or knowingly distorted, it was not possible to consistently apply them beneficially. The origin of the present dangerous rise of religious fundamentalism can probably be traced to this problem of narrow, non-understanding. This unfortunate development, among many other increasing problems now facing us, may be seen as a direct correlation between **the immutability of The Spiritual Laws** and **our refusal to heed them**. The solutions to **all** our problems lie **solely** in a voluntary adjustment to them in a conscious, correct and consistent way.

Simply put, we have no choice but to understand and apply The Spiritual Laws to every facet of human life and not believe we can formulate better principles that are as effective. For it would be foolish to imagine that human beings can improve on the Will of The Creator, as we ourselves are only products of those Laws. Chaos and confusion will always be the result of attempting to deviate from them. No one can evade or change them, and The Laws apply equally to all in the same measure. To rich and poor, the powerful and the weak, the clever and the stupid, to kings and slaves. The effects are the same on those who know the Law as on those who do not, and ignorance of them does not keep their effects at bay!

If man's laws are compared with Spiritual Law, we find that earthly laws differ from society to society whereas The Laws of Creation remain the same everywhere and are Eternal. Our laws are constantly in a state of review, and can even be changed by public opinion or dictatorial decree, so what may have been perfectly legal yesterday may not be so today. By contrast, Spiritual Law is immutable and unchangeable, and will forever remain so.

The cost, complexity and duration of trials in earthly law courts indicate quite conclusively that our laws are not simple to understand, and require lawyers who have needed to spend years of study to become conversant with them. Even then, however, there can be much disagreement over individual points of law. By comparison, The Laws of Creation are clear, concise and simple. Moreover, they are few in number, easily understandable, and do not require years of laborious study. They are alluded to in all the major religions and philosophies of the world's peoples. The chambers of Lawyers and Judges will contain row upon row of books of laws and statutes. The Eternal Laws, however, can be contained in just **one publication**.

The Eternal Laws have, as their infallible foundation, Justice, Love and Purity, and are therefore perfect in the dispensation of justice. By virtue of our present level of spiritual *immaturity* we, on the other hand, do not have such a benchmark. Despite the fact that we have many laws, we do not always see justice done. So-called "legal technicalities" permit clever lawyers to exploit the present "justice system" to set free people who have *actually* committed crimes. By contrast no one escapes The Spiritual Laws. Their infallible, automatic outworking ensures that Justice and Love are meted out in perfect balance at all times, even though not always immediately, or even apparently so. But meted out they always are!

The incorruptible nature of The Eternal Laws ensures that they will reign supreme. This means that in the determination of innocence or guilt in an earthly court of law, man's laws do not always offer protection or absolution should an innocent person be wrongly condemned and sentenced. The responsibility for that miscarriage of justice, however, will fall back on all those who contributed to it – as it must in all things. Attempting to shelter behind a veil of "fulfilling one's duty" in the ostensible application of justice via the Nation's laws matters not at all. We are all irrevocably tied to the consequences of our decisions, and a wrong conviction will eventually bring the inevitable reciprocal effect.

Judges and juries, then, have a particularly difficult task given the spiritually unhealthy state of our secular laws. Passing judgement according to such laws may satisfy the dictates of earthly society, but if the judgement is a transgression against The Laws of Creation, the judges are bound to reap the reciprocal effect of *their* spiritually-wrong decisions. For that reason, it should be in the interests of the judiciary to actively concern themselves with the knowledge of the Eternal Laws.

What should be seriously understood is the fact that the material worlds are *presently* in transition between one phase and another. Literally everything is in transition and upheaval, man and nature. Consequently man is being strongly compelled to heed these Laws under the increasing spiritual pressure currently being applied to all things. The effect of this pressure is seen in the accelerating breakdown of our society and the increasing problems globally. In short, man's time of formulating his own policies is at an end. We will now be forced to adjust to The Laws of Creation, or perish. This increasing pressure actually strengthens both the good and the bad.

Thus **the good** – *that which adjusts itself to The Laws* – **will flourish**. And the **bad or wrong** – *that which opposes The Laws* – **will collapse**. In this simple equation resides an infallible standard by which to measure events around us and to choose accordingly.

The Spiritual Laws of Creation, therefore, are relatively few in number. They are:

- **The Law of Movement**

- **The Law of Reciprocal Action**

- The Law of Attraction of Similar Species
- The Law of Spiritual Gravity
- The Law of Balance
- The Law of Rebirth
- Grace – A Gift of Divine Love

The living dynamic of the above principles is that their *inviolable effects* are *felt* as Laws whenever we oppose them. They *cease* to be Laws, and therefore become *helps*, when we abide by them. So by examining each of the Laws named, it will be shown that everything in Creation is interlinked and interdependent.[3]

How, then, should The Spiritual Laws be described? By examining philosophical, scientific, religious and spiritual works, clear and consistent reference to them can be found. Therefore they could be termed "Universal". Everyday observations of the natural world show this universality of The Laws in their working reality.

The philosopher Heraclitus (c.540-480 BC) of Ephesus in Asia Minor believed that this "universal reason" or "universal law" is something common to all and which guides not only every person but also everything that happens in nature. Yet he observed that instead of following this "higher guidance", most people lived by their individual beliefs. This "something", which was the source of everything, he called God or *logos* – meaning reason.

0.2 The Law of Movement!

0.2.1 Movement = Life.

Heraclitus also postulated a new concept; that of flux or change. He observed that everything flowed, everything is in constant flux and movement, and that nothing stands still. He expressed this concept of constant change by saying that "...you cannot step twice into the same river". The river changes because "...fresh waters are ever flowing in upon you". Heraclitus thought that this concept of

---

[3] A brief explanation is also offered on the vital characteristic of **Grace**. It is an feature lawfully linked with the perfect intermeshing of the Eternal Laws, commensurate with those decisions which strive for, or are directed toward, spiritual ascent.

flux "...must apply not only to rivers but to all things, including the soul of man". "Rivers and men exhibit the fascinating fact of becoming different and yet remaining the same. We return to the 'same' river although fresh waters have flowed into it, and the man is still the same person as the boy." (Philosophy History and Problems. Third Edition p 12/13.) Therefore, when we step into a river for the second time, neither we nor the river are the same.

Everything, literally everything, is in constant motion. Movement is the one activity that ensures the maintenance of life in all things. Without movement everything would become sluggish and eventually come to a complete standstill, a situation akin to death and disintegration. Therefore motion can be stated to be a most necessary principle throughout Creation. The higher and lighter the plane of Creation, the faster the motion. Conversely, therefore, the further away from the source of life, as for example in the Material Planes, the more sluggish the motion. As "movement" is thus a vital principle, all other laws can be said to operate within the parameters of this most important Law. However, the movement must be of the *right* kind and in harmony with all else if it is to bring benefit.

Imagine life in the Universe and on earth without the elemental activity of the Forces of Nature bringing movement. We observe the rotation of the earth each day to give the necessary circadian rhythm of day and night. The earth rotates around the sun to provide the four seasons. These in turn produce the different weather patterns needed for planting and harvesting. The motion of the winds ensures freshness and change where there might otherwise be staleness. Consider the moon's rotation around the earth, offering its different phases and bringing the rise and fall of the tides. Consider, also, the great ocean currents that constantly mix the waters of our "blue planet", and the movement of the continents over the liquid core of the earth in plate tectonics, instrumental in the formation of new lands. Constant movement equals constant renewal. Further out into the incomprehensible vastness of the observable universe, galaxies of immense size wheel and rotate billions of suns to the same primordial rhythm.

Science has long discovered that individual cells, molecules and atoms are "alive" with the constant movement of sub-particles, with each fitting perfectly into its ordained place to become part of the whole. And even in the microscopic sub-atomic world where the behaviour of quarks and neutrinos appear to circumvent all the known *scientific* laws they still, nevertheless, follow the dictates of

Universal Law. It is our non-understanding of those laws that force us to declare our lack of knowledge at such behaviour. The rocks of the earth, even though appearing to be solid, dense and lifeless, are also awhirl with active movement. A crystal-clear glass of clean water gives no hint of the motion of electrons, protons and neutrons in the structure and composition of either the glass or the water. Animal and human bodies have the same basic activity in their molecular structure also, whether living and breathing, or dead and decomposing.

The physical body, with which we are all familiar, signals to us the need for constant movement in order to remain healthy. In breathing we quite automatically accept the rise and fall of the chest as the lungs inhale and exhale. The heart pumps blood in necessary circulation throughout the body. Exercise keeps the body healthy and strong, inactivity weakens it. The demands of the toilet call us to the process of the elimination of body wastes at various times during the day. Even in supposedly restful sleep there is still the need for the body to change its position more often than we might be aware of during the sleep state. Everything must obey The Law of Movement if it is to remain healthy and not stagnate.

Rivers and streams remain fresh and oxygenated through movement. The world's great river systems yearly transport millions of tons of silt to form large, fertile deltas at their mouths. In manmade lakes where dams block the normal river flow to the point where the amount of draw off prevents any natural spillage, the impounded body of water still has movement between the vertical layers of water.

In the world of birds and fishes, lack of the right kind of necessary movement has resulted in the loss of certain abilities that some once possessed. For example, there are fish that are no longer able to withstand the currents and must remain near the bottom. Many birds in various parts of the world have become flightless through not having used their wings over a long period of time. These examples showing the principle of adaptation, with which biological scientists are familiar, are a consequence of The Law of Movement.

Up to this point we have only examined the physical effect of this Law. In the first instance, however, it is a Spiritual Law. Therefore, in the case of the physical body, each individual movement must first be "willed" by the spirit, because the spirit is the animating force, "the power pack", within each of us. This *signal* between spirit and body happens so quickly as to be virtually simultaneous and imperceptible in its time-lapse aspect.[4]

The activity of the natural world demands that every creature and plant must strive to maintain its place or perish. Spiritual activity must produce the same, and more, if there is to be growth and ascent. Therefore, effort must be expended if we wish to achieve anything of lasting value. We cannot sit back and expect wonderful things to just happen. Whether applied to the physical, mental or spiritual, laziness in any one area is a transgression against this Eternal Law. Moreover, the different kinds of activities – spiritual, intellectual and physical – must always be kept in proper balance. Without spiritual activity as a necessary counterpoise, physical and intellectual expenditure of effort will ultimately be worthless. We can extrapolate from this that a genuinely spiritual goal will always have furthering values that will never change and, by definition, be far-reaching and beneficial.

Present trends allow people to eagerly anticipate retirement after a lifetime of work. The thought of the remaining years of life spent in blissful inactivity appeals to many. Yet this offends against the Law too. Of course the elderly could not be expected to maintain the same level of activity that a much younger person might. Nevertheless, for the older body to maintain reasonable health, movement of the right kind is still necessary. Fortunately, current directions now see more and more of the elderly pursuing this beneficial course. The "acceptance of change" that time and development naturally bring under The Law of Movement permits one phase of life to flow into the next, for movement is designed to bring about *further* development.

Conversely, "workaholics", some professional sports people, and others engaged in constant frenetic activity actually transgress this Law and will eventually harm themselves. A sense of balance should be maintained in all that we do by adjusting to natural rhythms connected to The Law of Movement. Perhaps the latter day phrase, "Everything in moderation", is a sub-conscious reaction to the increasingly unnatural pace of modern society. In heeding The Law of Movement, we also need to obey The Law of Balance as well, for this Law is also a consequence of motion.

History's testament to the rise and fall of some of the great civilisations provides excellent examples of what occurs if the correct

---

[4]The "Spiritual" origin of humankind, thus that which pertains to the origin and nature of the human spirit and soul, is addressed in the Parent Book and in the Booklet – Whither Cometh Humankind (The Origins of Man) *Genesis and Science Agree!*

"spiritual" movement is not maintained. The rise to greatness can show the right kind of movement, whilst the disintegration process invariably indicates the opposite. The Law of Movement decrees that no one person, group or nation can simply stop and rest on past or even present glories. What has been achieved, if spiritually worthwhile, must be maintained or stagnation, retrogression and disintegration will quickly follow. In the same way, persons who have been publicly honoured by society should be required to maintain that position of honour.

The propensity of many to attempt to live in the past offends against The Law of Movement also. The current strong cultural trend in some ethnic communities to promote tribal links and/or a return to tribalism per se, clearly transgresses The Law of Movement in both the spiritual and material sense. The spiritual power and pressure inherent in this Law decrees that the tribal phase for any race is exactly that – just a phase. Consequently any beneficial outworking contained within the power of The Law of Movement for a people will be greatest when and where *correct movement* is undertaken. For certain ethnic groups, that would translate into leaving tribalism behind and moving toward becoming one nation, one people.

This does not mean that we should not assess history, or try to correct past wrongs. The Laws, however, require us, indeed command us, to *live* in the *present*. They further command us to strongly heed The Law of Movement – in the spiritual sense particularly – if there is not to be stagnation and retrogression.

Thus The Law of Movement decrees that absolutely nothing can stand still. Should a point of stagnation be reached, a new impetus must be developed to prevent the possibility of retrogression. Any new idea, though, should have, as its foundation, the application of Spiritual Law so that only upward movement is generated. For this Law will drive either upwards or downwards equally powerfully, exactly in accordance with the kind of decision taken.

0.3 The Law of Reciprocal Action!

0.3.1 Decisions Produce Consequences.

"Do not err; God cannot be deluded: for what a man sows, that he will also reap."

"If he sows for his sensuality, he will reap perdition; but

> *sowing for the Spirit, from the Spirit, he will reap eternal life."*

(Galatians 6:7-8, Fenton.)

The key word in the above Scriptures is **"will"**. It is not a word such as *perhaps*, for example, or *might*, or *maybe*, or *possibly*. No, the texts are quite unequivocal. They clearly state that we **"will"** reap what we sow! Other Bibles use the word "shall" in this context, but the meaning is obviously still the same.

In eastern religions the word "karma" is generally used to describe the very same effect/outcome. This particular word, however, unfortunately produces negative reactions in many Christians. Yet the very word perfectly represents the exact Law that Its Bringer, Jesus, taught. Thus:

> "*A knowledge of* **the iron law of karma** *encourages the earnest seeker to find the way of final escape from its bonds.*"

(Autobiography of a Yogi, Paramahansa Yogananda, p 563
Emphases mine.)

0.3.2 Faith Versus Works.

The theological argument of *faith* versus *works* can best be clarified using this "iron Law" as a guide. Faith is the primary aspect of a belief which strongly accepts that a particular thing is so and which therefore stems from a confident belief in the truth, value or trustworthiness of it. It is a belief, moreover, which does not rest on logical proof or material evidence. Faith, therefore, can perhaps be stated to be an implicit belief and trust in God and in the doctrines expressed in the Scriptures or other sacred works. Faith, however, even though a noble virtue, is nevertheless amorphous in its nature for its *actual* essence cannot be seen or touched. The New Testament documents many cases where faith, alone, produced miraculous outcomes around the presence of Jesus. The woman who believed that all she had to do was touch His robes to be healed, and the ones who stated that He had only to "...say the Word" and those for whom they sought healing *would* be healed. His acknowledgement: "Your faith has saved/healed you."

The story of the Captain who implored Jesus to heal his son whom he had left sick and dying at his home demonstrates **both** the faith paradigm **and** sure conviction. Believing implicitly that just The Word of The Son of God would heal his son brought forth a "surprised response" from Jesus. Matthew [8:10-11] records that He said to His followers:

> "Indeed, I tell you, I have never found such faith as this in Israel."

Faith in its sum and substance can therefore provide, and be, a powerful anchorage for one's religious beliefs, but it probably cannot be said to *be,* or *hold,* absolute conviction in the thing believed in. Faith, however, *should precede* **conviction**; that element of *sure and certain knowing* commonly derived from, but no longer *constrained by,* the faith paradigm itself.

Historically, great and wonderful works have been produced from and by faith, and the outworking of the great Law of **Sowing and Reaping** will automatically bring the appropriate "return effect" to the instigators and builders of those works. So remarkable blessings can derive from good works produced by faith alone.

If works are undertaken from **conviction**, however, – clearly accepting that that very word presupposes an *absoluteness of knowing about that which has wrought the conviction in the first place* – then the volition, the instigation and the building of the work/s proceeds with the concomitant sureness of knowing *exactly why* such a project is undertaken. Therefore such labour undertaken by either an individual or a group works *consciously* within the actual parameters of The Laws and their reciprocal outworking. Works produced through conviction, therefore, inherently carry within them a much stronger connection to the source of that particular certainty. Works produced by faith cannot inherently do so.

Faith possesses the *lesser value* of simply *believing it knows.*

Conviction, however, possesses *the sureness of knowing.*

In terms of the outworking of The Law of Reciprocal Action, then, the absolute perfection of The Spiritual Laws will return the exact reciprocal effect to both kinds of "builders" – whether through *faith* or *conviction*. In the final analysis, though, the faith/belief paradigm, which many in the Christian world promote as the only standard necessary for spiritual ascent, clashes diametrically with that which Jesus clearly stated:

> "**By their *works* you shall know them.**"

When told by His Disciples – whilst preaching in a synagogue – that His Mother and brothers were waiting outside for Him [emphases mine], Jesus declared:

> "Who is My mother, who is My brother? They are those who *carry out the Will of the Father*!"

The lament of Jesus over the little faith expressed by those of the race who were called to **support and follow Him** ring down through the centuries as an indictment on many today i.e., **"O ye of little faith."** Such paucity of faith during his life contrasted hugely with His great joy upon finding firm and unshakeable faith in He and His Mission from people not of that chosen race, such as the Roman Centurion.

How, then, should one carry out such **works**; through **faith**, or through **conviction**? Whose teachings should the well-meaning Christian follow? Present-day mainstream Church and Bible interpretation of Paul's ministry and philosophy has evidently and rather strangely concluded that Paul the Apostle taught that *faith, alone*, was sufficient. Jesus, on the other hand, *demanded* **works**. His admonition to "Take up the cross and follow Me" simply means that any believer in Him must *live The Laws*, and not simply pay lip service to them; thus *work*.

> **"I come not to overthrow the laws but to fulfil them."**
> – and – **"Go thou and do likewise."** – – (i.e., 'By My [**His**] example'.)

Did Paul live by 'faith, alone', or did he live by conviction? His amazing ministry bears unequivocal testimony to the fact that his **works** far transcended simple faith, for they were clearly imbued with the absolute **conviction** that can only derive from truly **knowing**.

The 'Christianised' 'Pauline philosophy' of 'faith, alone' – *which terribly distorts and denigrates Paul's great work* – now permeates a very large part of Christendom. It has unfortunately bequeathed to millions of Christians worldwide a spiritually dangerous mind-set that offers 'believers' little more than the 'broad easy path' Jesus warned against. To simply opt for faith, alone, without genuine works – even if only works to at least back up the faith aspect – fatally inculcates an acceptance that there is 'no need to do more'. Unfortunately, such an attitude basically derives from the unsound belief of many Christians that "He died for us", "for *our* sins".

In our view it is an element of, and an extrapolative excrescence basically formulated by Christian distortion of its so-called 'Pauline philosophy'.

There is obviously no doubt that Jesus died *because* of us! But the unshakeable belief of many that He died "for us" being sufficient to secure "a place in heaven" for them, logically ensures that the perfect and inviolable outworking of The Law of Sowing and Reaping cannot possibly extend its Grace and Blessings to such believers – **if** – it **is works that are demanded by Jesus, and thus by the Living Divine Laws!**

Consequently it would seem to be a very intelligent thing to choose to heed the *admonitions* of Jesus over Christendom's distorted 'Pauline philosophy'.[5]

The necessary transition from faith to conviction – from faith to works – can only thus derive from, firstly, the *recognition* of **The Spiritual Laws of Creation** and, secondly, their *serious application* in one's life.

Now, since all The Spiritual Laws can be designated as Natural Laws – which outworking and fulfilment we observe and experience in the totality of our lives each day – then it is vital to understand that the *infallible mechanism* for that outworking is actually the *inviolable perfection of The Laws themselves.* They are Laws whose validity, authority, perfection, and therefore absolute inviolability, derive from The Divine Perfection of The Creator Himself, and are thus Laws that, without flaw or deviation, return to us every nuance of every decision we make.

And because we sought conscious life and petitioned The Creator for it, The Spiritual Laws of Life, woven into the fabric of His Creation, are thus the Rules *by which we must live*. Through petitioning for conscious life, we were *irrevocably bound* to the *living reality* that the gift of free will *automatically* imbued us with the *personal responsibility* to exercise that gift correctly by heeding His Laws *and living accordingly*. A key Law by which the effect of our free-will inheritance is most clearly revealed and experienced is "**The Law of Reciprocal Action**".

A prime example of the damage that can be wrought through transgressing this particular Law may be clearly observed in the relatively recent episode of "mad cow disease" in Britain. Short-

---

[5] Chapter 5 of the Parent Book offers further clarification about key theological questions around the life and death of Jesus. Also in the Sister Booklet: Jesus! *His Birth, Death and Resurrection*

cut economic practices in British agriculture resulted in the concomitant emergence of a human equivalent of the disease through the consumption of contaminated meat and meat products from infected animals. This resulted in the terrible but necessary slaughter of many thousands of infected beasts.

The Laws of Creation ordain that herbivores such as cows and beef cattle should not consume food derived from their own kind. Meat and meat products are the ordained, natural food of carnivores, and the farming industry cannot arbitrarily *force* such a radical change in the diet of captive animals without expecting severe consequences. That shameful event produced a hard, "lawful" lesson for agricultural "science".

Should this kind of "animal husbandry" practice be continued with, perhaps that "hard lesson" may still yet manifest in a globally devastating way. The discovery of *prions*, the strange and potentially lethal *protein agent* perhaps implicated in the *brain-eating diseases*, CJD, BSE, sheep scrapie and *kuru* (from New Guinea), are now a great concern. Over the past few decades, American and Australian scientists observing and researching these diseases have noted the striking similarities between them. At the same time, they have also noted the increasing incidences of variants of the disease, particularly among the young.

The Book of Job (34:11), in succinct truth about this particular Law, perfectly states the consequential reality of such foolish "science" in just six blunt words.

"But man's actions return on himself."

Science notates the essence of this very Law thus:

"For every action, there is an equal and opposite reaction."

However, what is probably not accepted or even known is that there is not just simply an *"equal*, opposite reaction", but a reaction that is always "lawfully imbued" with *greater power* ***in the "return"***. It is thus very much more than might be expected to result from the originating decision.

In the case of our example of the moment, the possibility that "mad cow disease" may have crossed the species barrier to infect humans should be regarded as unequivocal proof that The Spiritual Laws, which ultimately manifest as physical Laws, cannot be transgressed without **serious** consequences. The full potential horror of "mad cow disease" may still be a little way off, for the great uncertainty is whether or not there may be a large pool of infected people quietly moving through an unknown incubation period.

According to research published in the British Medical Journal around September 20th 2002, more than 7000 Britons could face an increased risk of contracting the human form of mad cow disease. In this example alone we can clearly note that **The Law of Reciprocal Action**, as with all The Spiritual Laws, necessarily supports every other Law as a part of all processes and outcomes.

But even with such obvious warning signs now clearly present, science, in its dangerously flawed mind-set that it can change the lawful processes of natural development against the Ordination of The Creator, are slowly taking this aberrant experimentation to what must be recognised and understood as being levels of actual insanity.

The position adopted by this particular branch of science states that by inserting human genes into cows, milk will be produced that will ostensibly heal various kinds of diseases in human beings. Such a misguided view, however, fails to even *begin to understand* that if we desire better outcomes in *all areas* of life – *including health* – then we must heed the very Laws of Life. **That** is how we gift to ourselves optimum health.

Perhaps the greater danger, however, lies in the insidious nature of the seductive, emotional propaganda that is used to sell the whole idea. That emotionalism ultimately feeds on the fear of millions of the sick globally whom GE science claims could be saved from so-called premature death if these "life-saving" techniques were permitted. The other beguiling aspect lies in the fact that not only are many political "leaders" hell-bent on supporting this branch of "science", but even within indigenous communities of the world there are those who have been seduced by this new and dangerous direction.

An interesting paradox arises here. The sophisticated technology of this particular branch of western scientific thinking – which regards the cow as solely a factory unit for the production of by-products to pamper people who, for the most part, have refused to live correctly healthily anyway – have absolutely no idea of *either* The Laws which govern all science, which *ultimately constrains all wrong science* anyway, or of the *life-force* present in all animals. In striking contrast to that position, many millions in India view cows in a totally different light. Even though wrongly revering them as sacred, they nevertheless understand that their value lies in the animal just as it is *in its natural state* – as a giver of milk as food unadulterated by flawed science. At least, that is the general position at this time.

The one note of sanity in the West thankfully lies in the swelling volume of people and groups utterly and implacably opposed to any such aberrant deviation away from the complete naturalness of the Perfection of The Laws of GOD, the earthly expression of which we may note in The Laws of Nature. Or, to use a better understood term, the "Natural Laws"! And no earthly science can ever oppose them with arrogant impunity. Of course, there is always a period of time for such experimentation to run its particular course, for free will is never taken from us.

If the world's humanity were to truly spiritually awaken, then implacable opposition to all GE technology would be understood to be spiritually, and thus *scientifically*, correct. It would not be regarded as some kind of aberrant "green-fringe fanaticism" as it presently is. For we already have, among other disturbing incidents, the lessons of lower yields for GE crops, and the increasing spread of GE contamination away from original release points. Gary Goldberg, when CEO of the American Corn Growers Association (ACGA), spoke about the harm GE technology has caused US farmers:

> "**This is a case of if we knew then what we know now, American farmers would not have been so easily convinced that GE crops were the way to go.** Our land has become contaminated with GE pollution that we cannot control or remove from our environment. Conventional farms are being contaminated, and we have no choice of GE or non-GE crops. **None of the promises have come true and it is time for farmers to understand that the promises that have been made and will continue to be made will not come true either.** We are losing export markets... Those markets can be filled by [other] farmers..."
>
> (Physicians and Scientists for Responsible Genetics. Parentheses mine.)

But even facts such as those outlined here are still not yet sufficient to convince the proponents of this dangerously-flawed foolishness – the scientists, the politicians and those people who subscribe to it – that any kind of experimentation with the actual genome of humans and animals to try to bring about a genetic modification or mutation will be far more devastating than just simple plant modification.

For whilst each species of the plant kingdom has its own specific genetic code, which gives it its particular perfection of function and form, the plants themselves do not possess the same *kind of life force* that humans and animals have. And it is that *specific kind of inner animation* that has driven the development of humans and given the many and varied species of animals their unique place in the world. Without any input from human "science", the evolution and development of all life forms has proceeded in accordance with a plan that permits the absolute perfection of each. It is a plan that GE earth-sciences could not even begin to emulate, yet arrogantly believes it can improve upon.

Such a serious transgression is not at all difficult to prophesy against, for that will forever and always be the outcome of working against The Laws of life in any case. The final outcome will therefore reveal itself in the reciprocal effect/s that each group – the supporters and the opposers – will one day subsequently receive. That, we can be sure, will be a "devastating return" for one side; that of its supporters.

At a more natural level, a brief examination of this effect in the natural world will clearly show even the youngest gardener that if he wishes to harvest corn, he must plant corn, and if he wants to grow beans, he must plant beans. What would be the result if The Laws were inconsistent and we were always uncertain as to what the sown seed would produce? Total confusion. And there is no confusion in The Spiritual Laws of Creation. Therefore, as it reveals its absolute certainty in the garden, so can the same certainty be observed in all other kinds of "sowing".

Closely connected with this fact should be the realisation that we therefore do not necessarily "***reap in the same season that we sow***". Thus, whilst the time difference between sowing and reaping, or cause and effect, usually has set periods between the sowing and harvesting of seed for earthly food crops, no such set time-period can be determined for the sowing and harvesting of "spiritual" seed. The Spiritual Laws alone determine the precise time of such "returns".

Within the various races and religions of the world, moreover, the natural Laws take no account of an individual's colour or belief. Rice sown by a white, brown or black man will produce exactly the same as for a yellow man. In the same way, wheat sown by a Jew, a Christian, a Buddhist, a Moslem, a Hindu, a Pagan, or an Atheist, will return only wheat at harvest time. As previously stated, this earthly effect well reflects the fact that this Law, along with all the other Spiritual Laws, grants no special bias or favour to any particular race or religion. Neither should it be expected to do so.

The perfection of such Laws absolutely guarantees that they cannot possibly do anything other than dispense Perfect Justice to all men. Thus, if an Atheist or a Pagan sows goodness, they are lawfully bound to receive goodness; as will a Christian Bishop, a Hindu Monk, a Moslem Imam, or a Native Shaman. Therefore, it is not necessarily a man's belief or religion that determines whether he will *ascend* or not, it is **how he is in his inner being**. It is the "Spiritual volition" of his inner nature toward all that surrounds him, both the seen and unseen, that greatly determines the outcome.

Spiritually then, it would be wrong to think that membership of a particular religion or sect would guarantee "good returns" or *reaping* – or even salvation. The purpose of all religion should be to help to correctly interpret The Will of God as expressed in The Laws of Creation, thus showing us how we are to carry out His Will. If it can do that, then it fulfils its place, for religions should be recognised as means to an end and not ends in their own right. As previously noted, the dangerous rise of religious fundamentalism illustrates too narrow an interpretation of just "earthly religious law".

Now, since the current premise under the particular Law being discussed here is exactly that of "reaping what one has sown", but from the spiritual viewpoint overall, it is necessary to have a mechanism whereby this "Spiritual" aspect also produces "physical reaping". Anecdotal evidence from American medical research has shown that concentrated thoughts directed to a sick patient can directly influence the healing process of that patient. Thus what spiritual and even philosophical thinking have been saying for a very long time actually happens. In simple terms, good thoughts directed to a patient can hasten the healing process whilst bad thoughts can lengthen it.

The best-selling "Sophie's World" (p 193) offers a light-hearted insight regarding this quandary.

> A Russian astronaut and a Russian brain surgeon were once discussing religion. The brain surgeon was a Christian but the astronaut was not. The astronaut said: "I've been out in space many times but I've never seen God or angels." And the brain surgeon said, "And I've operated on many clever brains but I've never seen a single thought".

Neither view can conclusively prove that one or the other exists materially of course... And that is as it should be for neither are material in form. Nevertheless, in accordance with Spiritual Law, exist they do! Therefore, what might the above two anecdotes suggest to us?

They strongly indicate that thoughts, *despite* their invisible nature, *do* have the power to influence our lives, and produce visible effects. Our thoughts must thus have to be much more than empty vaporous things. To be able to influence in such a way, they must necessarily be imbued with some kind of inherent power. All the great Spiritual Teachings, even from ancient times, strongly advise to constantly strive to think good and pure thoughts. The emotive words of love, beauty, compassion and kindness automatically arouse in us vastly different feelings from words such as hate, selfishness, envy and bitterness. This small example, where the outworking of Spiritual Law is concerned, should serve to show that language alone is not the deciding factor here. The actual *volition* of the *producer* of the spoken word very strongly determines what is ultimately released *from* him "into the world".

Thus every thought we think, every word we speak produces a "form" that actually lives. The thought or word produces the actual form of it i.e., thoughts or words of hate or bitterness will produce those forms, **irrespective of whatever language is used as the medium of production**. Forms of love and harmony etc. are produced by the same mechanism. Just because such forms cannot always be seen does not mean that they do not exist, for they can certainly often be felt. Neither can they simply and conveniently disappear. No, the forms that we produce, that we have given birth to, live on until such time as they return to us under this iron Law of Reciprocal Action.[6]

We, as the individual originators, are the *owners* of them. They are ours. Moreover, our thoughts naturally affect our immediate environment, family and friends. We may note how refreshing it feels to enter the dwelling of a family who live a happy, balanced, harmonious life. Contrast that with a household racked by jealousy, hate and bitterness. A thoroughly unpleasant atmosphere, which is immediately perceived, pervades the place. The constant production of the corresponding *forms* "fills" the house. **It becomes their home too.**

This process then, can be viewed as *Spiritual sowing*. We "sow"

---

[6]What happens to them whilst on their "journey" will be explained later on in this Essay under the effects of "The Law of Attraction..."

through thoughts, words, volition, deeds and actions. It is precisely through this simple mechanism that humankind *forms and forms and forms*. Indeed, through the inherent free will of our spiritual nature, we are **unable** to stop forming. Therefore, if our thoughts are always good, we must naturally receive good returns. If they are constantly evil, that is what will be eventually received. If our thoughts and actions change between good and evil, we will receive mixed fortunes incorporating both those aspects. In this infallible mechanism lies perfect justice! We should all live by the admonition:

"As you wish men to do to you, do the same to them."

(Luke 6:31, Fenton.)

Such practical wisdom was given for our benefit under the knowledge of The Law of Reciprocal Action. Therefore, the greater strength and benefit will always lie in doing good deeds. The key to solving the many problems that beset us rests in the operation and understanding of this Law for it decrees that we cannot do anything other than continually *produce* our personal *works*. Yet because we cannot "physically" see them, it is difficult to accept that such a process might be possible.

Since thoughts have the power to influence, in cases where people act differently to their actual intentions i.e., as a "wolf in sheep's clothing" etc., the Law of Sowing and Reaping absolutely ensures that the "true" actions, including related thoughts and volition, are still all exactly weighed. The same inflexible process takes place with people who make donations to organisations for some kind of personal gain or publicity, but do not accept or share their aims and ideals. This attitude is actually one of hypocrisy and is judged accordingly because of its base level of calculative premeditation. A common Biblical quote clarifies the process perfectly. From Matthew 7:1:

Judge not, lest ye be judged!

However, because so few people have the ability to clearly assess the true intentions of others, it is often difficult to know whether intuitive "gut feelings" are correct, simply because a person's appearance or actions may belie his true volition. And even whilst seeing his actions and hearing his words, we may still not know his real motives.

However, if the term "judge" *means* to "weigh" or "consider", then the points for and against any particular issue should *not* be seen as a transgression of the above Scripture. Clearly we are meant to utilise our reason, intelligence and intuition to consider whether a particular thing is good or not. Therefore judging the actions of a person or an issue is vastly different from **passing judgement** on the person or issue. In this light, the *same* Scripture from Matthew in Fenton's translation of the Bible offers a clearer and better interpretation.

*"**Condemn not**, so that you may not be **condemned**."*

Now whilst we have examined the mechanism that "produces our reaping", it is necessary to clarify the very important *reciprocal extension* of the process. The ostensibly enigmatic Scripture from the Book of Hosea 8:7, Fenton, actually offers perfect clarification. [All emphases mine.]

*"And as they have sown only Wind, **the Whirlwind alone shall they reap**."*

Thus, in the world of nature, each seed that is planted produces a huge multiple of the same at maturation or harvest time. In some cases, in the millions. Some crops require only a few months between sowing and harvesting. In the forest industry, tree crops take many years to mature before felling. Depending on when planting took place, they may not be ready in a given lifetime. Even different varieties of the same kind of crop may mature at different intervals.

How should this be related to the great Spiritual Law of Sowing and Reaping? Quite simply, our spiritual sowing of either good or bad thoughts and deeds also returns a multiple of the same, in close association with another Eternal Law – "The Law of Attraction of Similar Species" – hence the truth of "reaping the whirlwind" in the previous Biblical quote. The differences in the time frame of crop maturation also have their equivalent in the spiritual too, and apply equally to the thoughts, words, deeds, volition, and even prayers of people.

The outworking of all these factors provide the answer as to why sudden misfortune can visit itself on a "good person", or good fortune arrive to a well known "waster". That is also the reason why someone who is totally debased may not receive his personal "whirlwind" until very much later in life, or even after earthly death. Rest assured, though, it will come to him. Not, however, in the same measure as he meted out to others, but under the additional severity of the *whirlwind constant*.

If this were not the case i.e., without any form of ultimate justice, there would be little point in bothering with the good. In the jungle that would develop, it would be easier to simply "take whatever one wanted".

In this regard the following Scripture from Hebrews 10:30 is more easily understood:

"PUNISHMENT IS MINE, I [THE LAW] WILL REPAY."

(Parenthetic addition mine.)

Thus, the Eternal Laws automatically keep track of all transgressors and, at the ordained time for that person, dispense the appropriate justice.

This does not mean, however, that we should not punish wrongdoers through our earthly justice system, otherwise there surely would be chaos. It simply means that nothing is missed in Creation, nothing can be hidden, and no individual can "get away" with any crime against The Spiritual Laws. The reciprocal effect, moreover, will always be greater than the strength of the original volition or deed under the outworking of the *whirlwind constant*. This process should offer some comfort as we observe more horrifying events and crimes that would have been unthinkable even a short while back, and which greatly increase in number and degree of brutality. Therefore the rule of law must be upheld at all times, as it should reflect our recognition of the "Higher Laws" along with a desire to build the right kind of society. Humankind's societal/religious "guidelines", however, need to fully accord with, and be adjusted to, those "Higher Laws".

It should also be a simple matter to deduce that we can only reap what we have *personally* sown. We cannot simply "sow" for others, or "reap" for them either, not even for a loved one. So a person constantly striving to do good and who receives bad experiences *apparently unfairly*, should understand that he will have given cause for it at some point in the past. As difficult a concept as this may be to accept, it *is* the causal reality of many of our problems. There is then nothing to be gained by bemoaning one's fate for this only increases the sense of burden and hardship. Recognition and acceptance of this lawful process, however, then connects us to the outworking of **Divine Grace**.[7]

In the global sense both our earthly home and the creatures upon it were given to humankind to nurture and protect; to take only what was required. Look at the the earth today, however? The story is glaringly obvious. Poisoned and pillaged in a mind-set of rapacious, selfish greed under the name of progress and *good economic strategy*. Unfortunately, because such practices ultimately impact on all eco-systems, it is now time for global humanity to "pay the ferryman". Yet the price may prove to be well beyond our ability to pay. Learning the "Rules" and living by them may perhaps go some way toward lessening the cost. It will still be very high, however, as that cannot be changed now – though it can perhaps be reduced.

There must, however, be a truly genuine desire to want to change, to seek something better. Superficiality in this case will simply ensure not just more of the same, but increasingly severe "reaping". For, as with all of The Spiritual Laws, this particular Law operates from the smallest, even apparently insignificant individual happenings, to far-reaching global decisions and events made collectively and subsequently "reaped".

Because the impact of "returning fate" may offer no apparent reason why, it is easy to rail against misfortune or bad luck, or to curse the fates and demand an end to hardship. And then, in times of deep pain with seemingly no way out, to desperately seek help in prayer. In my personal experience, *"when the chips are down"* virtually *everyone* calls out for **THE MAN!** There are few who will not seek help at such times. This inner recognition, most often brought about by painful experiences, should help us to understand that the reaping of bitter fruits once sown should be seen as the best possible *spiritual* reminder that *we have strayed from the path ordained by The Creator*.

If our understanding of the Eternal Laws and how we stand in relation to them is then examined honestly and in genuine humility, such an assessment can only help us to grow spiritually. Through this process the lessons needing to be learned can be more readily identified. Consequently, as the necessary adjustments are made whereby only good seeds are sown, the Law of Sowing and Reaping will ensure a good return at the ordained time. Thus there should be less thought of hard, cruel, or undeserved fate. Yet neither should we be totally fatalistic about our lot in life. *It is in our*

---

[7]The ramifications of this particular principle are examined later in this Booklet.

power to change it – at any time.

Of course, change may not come overnight, but stubbornly refusing to change for the better will absolutely guarantee that *nothing* will change or, indeed, *can* change. The Laws of Creation actually do provide the means for happiness or misery. What is "Willed" from above for all human spirits is peace and happiness, through the understanding of Spiritual Law. What one receives, however, depends solely upon ***individual choice.***

The question or problem of the "evil within man" and/or how evil arose in the world – so long a point of debate – has its primary explanation within this Law. It is simply a free-will choice, which we all inherently make in any case. And irrespective of whether the particular choice is made consciously and intentionally, or in total ignorance of this law, the Law of Sowing and Reaping ***will***, nevertheless, ***always deliver the consequences***.

In Cicero's "The Nature of the Gods", a simple and logically correct explanation is offered. In this particular discourse about the opposing views of Christianity and Stoicism, Thomas Godless asks Lactantius four questions on this subject. [Italics mine.]

> "My first difficulty", he said, "is that you do not seem to have been any better able than the Stoics to solve the problem of evil. How is the existence of pain and evil in the world compatible with your view that the world is under the care of an infinitely powerful and infinitely loving God?"
>
> To which Lactantius replied, "Thomas, I give you two answers. First, if Christianity offers men reconciliation with God, it is not required to solve every intellectual difficulty. But secondly, Christianity does provide a better answer to this age-old problem than Stoicism, because Stoicism is in principle deterministic, whereas the Christian God has given *freedom of choice to man...* He wants all things to serve him, not as automata but by free choice; but this gift of freedom involves the risk that man will *choose evil rather than good*. If God refrains from punishing the wicked in this world, that is a sign not of his powerlessness, but of his magnanimity. Epicurus insisted on human freedom, but at the expense of the gods' reality; the Stoics insisted on divine omnipotence, but at the expense of human freedom. Christianity allows for both."

Despite the *intellectual* brilliance with which the Greek and Roman philosophers were able to debate the pros and cons of major issues such as life and death and good and evil; without the knowledge of The Spiritual Laws of Creation to ultimately define the lawful processes under which all events have their beginning, life and end, all their philosophic musings had to remain exactly that. For the final key to the puzzle was not available to them at that time. That notwithstanding, the long line of philosophic thought in many ways did provide the necessary step for the much later entry and recognition – at least for some – of the **All** of Spiritual Truth and Law.

Thus, in this particular Law is fulfilled the fate or karma of humankind, and offers the solutions to the terrible tragedies which we witness today. Through the increasing spiritual power now entering the Material Part of Creation, all the deeds of thousands of years past are pressured to a quicker, final release, thereby also accelerating the *natural catastrophes*.

This *relentless pressure* and its attendant global events will not cease until all past cycles have closed, the deeds returned to their owners to face, and all opposition to the Eternal Laws has been removed. Then a new era will be ushered in, a time of genuine peace and happiness. Only for those of the world's people, however, who have genuinely striven for the good.

Decisions Produce Consequences.

That is the subsequent but perfectly lawful effect of: **The Law of Reciprocal Action!**

0.3.3 Attitude to the Suffering.

Given the obvious ramifications of the previous Law, it might be thought that we advocate total disregard for the plight of those in desperate straits. If, as is stated, people do bring suffering on themselves through non-observance of The Laws and that they are solely responsible for their plight, should compassion be shown for them? Are they not simply reaping what they have sown in this earth-life, or perhaps an earlier one? And do they therefore deserve to be helped? The simple answer to virtually all aspects of the overall question is yes!. Compassion and kindness are virtues that, if given selflessly, can only bring a good return to the giver. For the Law of Sowing and Reaping should clearly show the need to do good at all times.

"*Do unto others...*" should be one of the key factors governing our way of life. It is difficult to imagine that anyone would actually want others to visit harm or evil upon them, yet there are so many who seem to have little compunction in wishing that on others. That is the way of the coward, and clearly the way of much of today's world. It is not the path of nobleness, which is synonymous with true and genuine spirituality. Neither is it the way of **the genuine warrior**, for a true warrior will reflect those higher qualities and virtues. Employing genuine spirituality from out of the **true** knowledge as both his *primary* weapon and shield, he will fight for, and protect and defend, the weak, the helpless and the downtrodden.

Any good works we do, we do solely for ourselves since the fruits of our deeds return to us as multiples of our original sowing under the aegis of the *whirlwind constant*. The possibility of helping sufferers should therefore be regarded as an opportunity to do good, to "sow good seeds". The cause of the person's suffering should not be our concern. In short, we should not "pass judgement". Given the general nature of human beings, most judgements are based on externals anyway. And a superficial assessment may belie the true situation. However, help given *should not be one-sided*, for that will not help the sufferer in the long term.

In any case the perfection of The Laws automatically ensures that should a sufferer *not* deserve help, or should he need such experiencing to change his ways, then no one will cross that person's path who might be in a position to give help. Conversely, any necessary "crossing of paths" could mean that a connective origin might lie somewhere in the past e.g., as a "debt owed". In this case two opportunities are given for two different souls to expiate a possible past karmaic connection, sever it, and thus become free. If such an opportunity is not recognised, then, quite obviously, *the debt and connection remain*.

The inviolability of Spiritual Law means that all human beings will necessarily have ties to many people, and some will be to other races. Yet all will need to be resolved, even if the individual has no knowledge of such connections, or proffers cynical disbelief at such an idea. For the justness of The Laws will ensure that individual paths will cross at the appropriate time for any such bonds to be severed. Given the increasing spiritual pressure being relentlessly applied to the earth and all the affairs of men in this time of final accounting, a superficial or cynical outlook or lifestyle will not be conducive to correct or timely recognition. Just as our past free-will decisions irrevocably bind us to the origin of all "returning karma" today so, too, are we offered the free choice to unbind ourselves from them when the opportunity arises. Conversely we are equally free to remain shackled.

Free-will permits us the choice of what we will sow in thought, word or deed. The outworking of the Law of Sowing and Reaping then returns to us a multiple harvest, in just accordance with *the whirlwind constant*.

The strange and inexplicable notion that we somehow do not possess the inherent human attribute of free-will is perfectly logical and understandable to believe in the light of so much suffering on earth. Nonetheless, it is **precisely** that *perfection in logic* in this **Iron Law of Reciprocity** that is the *driving mechanism* responsible for all suffering. It is suffering *reaped*, however, **through our decisions and actions solely**, and not through the operation of some mindless and unpredictable arbitrary force as many foolishly believe. Therefore, the authors of the very many books questioning the so-called injustices of life need only familiarise themselves with The Laws, particularly **The Law of Reciprocal Action**, to understand how and why free-will *is* the human reality!

Certain kinds of books, such as "The God Delusion" by Professor Richard Dawkins, basically reject any notion of free-will. Precisely that rejection, however, ultimately reveals the fatuity of human thinking. In the final analysis the *actual delusion* is centred around the inane belief that "human knowledge", alone, can determine the how and why of *every single facet of life*. That, of course, is plain and simple nonsense deriving solely from "human arrogance".

0.3.4 "Ten Men Will Take Counsel And It Will Come To Nought."

Isaiah 8:10. Thus spake the Great Prophet thousands of years ago in *one* of his warnings to humankind of just *one* of the sure signs of the *end-time demise* of human institutions. A time when it would become glaringly-obvious that *unworkable* human law, ideas, opinions, national self-interest, greed – and fear – would finally herald the impending complete collapse of human societies right across the globe.

The spectacle of riots and protests outside the venue of the UN "Climate Change Summit" in Copenhagen, December, 2009, gave clear voice to Isaiah's sure prophecy. And that was only *outside* the venue. Inside – where key discussions took place amongst numerous international officials – the *human* temperature was just as heated; where genuine consensus for *nurturing* the planet which *nurtures us* collapsed into recrimination, blame and self-interest. Headlines: 'Confusion and anger at Climate Change Summit'.

The largest ever gathering of international leaders [192 Nations] "...failed to reach a binding agreement". While some larger 'economies', particularly the US, pushed for consensus in some areas, many smaller Nations felt 'disappointed', and 'excluded from deal'. Denounced by smaller countries and amid warnings that "...it does not go far enough"; one US official stated: "Deal not enough to fight climate change." "No country is really satisfied with [the] deal."

Why should anyone be surprised at that outcome? Our very human condition at this juncture in our evolutionary journey simply *precludes* any hope of a genuinely equitable agreement to fairly share what are now dwindling resources amongst an ever burgeoning human population. For what the richer first-world countries *currently* possess, all others now demand as a matter of right.

The most necessary attribute of **wisdom** seems not to exist in the mentality of negotiators such as those at the Copenhagen conference representing the various countries and peoples of the world. Not any kind of far-seeing spiritual wisdom encompassing the very life-essence of **Creation-Law**; but, as in the past, always the short-term 'consensual-fix' ostensibly designed to overcome any and all objections. In the case of the "Copenhagen Summit", 2009, however, [universally accepted as a 'failure'], serious polarising rifts clearly emphasised the *power* of Isaiah's Calling to *warn* humanity — even from the long-distant past!

> The "Earth" also is *defiled* under the *inhabitants* thereof; because they have
> ***transgressed*** the "Laws",
> ***changed*** the decrees,
> ***broken*** the everlasting covenant.
>
> (Isaiah 24:5, Emphases mine.)

In 1854 Chief Seattle of the Duwamish addressed Governor Isaac Stevens and gave what is probably *inadequately described* as; "...the most beautiful and profound statement on the environment ever made". Now preserved for posterity; his *full* address should *especially* be prominent in the homes and work places of all politicians, bankers, 'money-men', CEO's, Boards of Directors, and all who aspire to so-called 'leadership'. In truth, if we *really* wish to have any kind of planet worth living on, Chief Seattle's great wisdom should be made mandatory reading from an early age for *all* peoples of *all* races!

Culled from his more comprehensive statement, the following few lines appropriately encapsulate the foolishness displayed by national and perhaps even ethnic self-interest at 'Copenhagen, 2009'.

> "Whatever befalls the earth, befalls the sons of the earth. If men spit upon the ground they spit upon themselves.
> This we know, the earth does not belong to man, man belongs to earth. Man did not weave the web of life, he is merely a strand in it. Whatever he does to the web, he does to himself.
> One thing we know, which the White Man may one day discover – our God is the same God. You may think now that you own Him as you wish to own our land, but you cannot.
> The earth is precious to Him and to harm the earth is to heap contempt on it's Creator.
>
> ***Continue to contaminate your bed and one night you will suffocate in your own waste.***"

(Emphasis mine.)

At this present time in humankind's evolutionary journey; in ecological terms we stand on the edge of an abyss. Unless we change our thinking and attitude towards the single, great interconnected-organism that permits us life *down here* – **Planet Earth** – the majority of humankind will shortly topple into that widening chasm. The corporate 'gurus' call it scaremongering or similar. They will also say we can solve all the problems that 'global warming' is wreaking on human societies now, never mind the exponential effect already evident. The equation is quite simple.

Planet Earth can only give as much of its *life-energy* as its own 'constantly-renewing ecology' will *actually allow*.

Economies, societies and cultures of global humanity ***must therefore respect and embrace Earth's 'natural program'***. The resources of the planet, though finite, can still be constantly sustainable if output, or *extraction*, equals input, or *correct conservation*. Earth's biosphere does *not* possess an 'endless-growth mechanism' for we 'lemming-like' humans now numbering in the ***'too-many' billions***.

So, when extraction of resources *far exceeds* Earth's sustainable threshold just to fuel growth and consumerism for obscene profit – as has been the case with Western capitalism since the Industrial Revolution – degradation of the planet's 'life-system' is the inevitable result. Thus, Earth's 'supplies' are now in serious deficit. And that deficit is growing exponentially under impossible yet nonetheless precisely-related increasing human demands deriving from explosive population-growth. And therein lies the heart of the problem – *too many people*. To this writer's knowledge, only *one* internationally-syndicated commentator – Gwynne Dyer – has had the courage to state this clear fact.

Notwithstanding China's attempts to limit population growth there, for most governments, religions, cultures, ethnic groups etc., the idea of publicly promoting some kind of reduction mechanism for human population growth is, perversely, almost akin to 'suicide'. Yet that is *exactly* the outcome for our growing billions, *for we have had neither the courage nor the genuine inclination to institute real and necessary change.*

So now: More growth, more consumerism, more waste, more immigration into wealthy Western economies to fuel this insidious and fatally-compromised, never-ending, insane carousel called **Capitalism** degrades and finally destroys increasingly-fragile, global eco-systems. Concomitantly, also, destruction of *excessive* 'first-world' type lifestyles, and the *culling* of Earth's population.

Even a fool can understand that!

Should that sound warning bells for the political and economic 'movers and shakers'? Most definitely! However, as evidenced by more rapid degradation and destruction of more and more eco-systems, 'they', for this short time of 'pregnant pause' anyway, are obtusely blind and deaf to the glaring reality of the moment. The awakening, though, *will come soon* – hard and suddenly.

What drives this mad carousel? One word: **Capitalism** – *American brand capitalism.* And, of course, its twin partner in crime; the **share-market** – the shareholders of which 'continually demand' larger and larger 'profit-returns' no matter how derived or who or what suffers for 'their' dividend.

For there are more than enough well-documented cases where Western capitalism has destroyed living standards of whole groups of people by simple *abandonment* for a cheaper work-force and/or tax break elsewhere; after the initial foray to *raise* living standards by offering paid employment to produce the 'corporate goods' and its share-holder profits. And, too often, also, obscenely high earnings for such 'selfish-thinking' people – the C.E.O.'s and 'Boards of Directors'. Even the increasing involvement of 'Global Corporates' in the beneficially-growing 'Fair-Trade Movement' has only been seeded by consumers who are primarily *not* their share-holders.

Previously *seriously-exploiting* Third-world Nations for very large profits, it was never an altruistic decision for the *benefit* of the Third-world on the part of at least the greater majority of the larger 'Corporates'. No! The 'awakening and greening' of the Western consumer has forced the 'uncaring greedy' of the Corporate world to begin to change their ways, for 'large-profit economics' is the name of their game here too.

And what, in the final analysis, drives 'Corporate-capitalism', the real power that 'calls the shots' for Governments and global societies? One word – 'petrodollars'! Petroleum is the one single commodity and 'force' which has both permitted and driven capitalist expansion and its concomitant human demographic explosion from about one billion at the turn of the 20th century to numbers that can no longer be 'fed and watered' adequately in the first decade of the 21st century – over six and a half billion.

I hear cries of horror and *dismissive-derision* from all capitalists. Yet even the most rabid of them **cannot deny** that **by its very nature** capitalism **demands** growth and more growth to survive, thus generating the profits **needed** to fuel **more growth** for **still greater profits**. And only with *sufficient* petroleum supplies can *that kind of growth* be maintained. In a brutally-objective assessment of the impact of such an ethos and **associated monetary system** on human and natural life; in the final analysis it is quite simply insane – because *in its present form and application it is completely unsustainable.*

And so, in the 21st century, more financial institutions, national and worldwide, have "...bitten the dust". **Many more will follow, until all that refuse to abandon their present 'as-piritual practices' collapse completely.**

As we strongly assert in this Booklet: The *increasing Spiritual pressure* – or *spiritual-stranglehold* – now being *exponentially-applied* to all the affairs of men actually strengthens both the good and the bad. Thus *the good* – or that which adjusts itself to **The Law** – *will prosper.* And *the bad or wrong* – that which **opposes** Creation-Law – **will collapse.**

In that truism we have an infallible standard by which to measure events around us and to choose accordingly.

The greater insanity here is that the economic 'growth-engine model' based on 'oil', 'black gold', has finally run its course. In terms of human history, 'petroleum-power' represents just a short steep spike on the graph of human habitation on Planet Earth. Yet in that brief historical period now spiking downwards exponentially were fought the most destructive wars in our history. Global wars *only* made possible because of oil to drive the war machines and the industries which conceived and built them in their vast numbers, and which grew the societies that brought forth the men to man them.

"A Crude Awakening": Exactly the right Documentary – which should be mandatory viewing for all – for the latter half of the first decade of the 21st century, where, despite denials by certain Western Governments and Petro-chemical industry 'gurus', oil output from virtually all of the major suppliers has already peaked. Soon, the battle will begin for what is still left. The strong will simply take from the weak in what will be a destructive and desperate struggle by the major economic and Military powers of the Northern hemisphere to control oil to maintain their growth and/or superpower status.

For without oil, modern societies simply cannot be sustained. Technologically advanced societies and economies must and will suffer irretrievable collapse. In its train, all the attendant anarchical horrors *automatically deriving from* major and widespread collapse of *once-stable* societal support systems and infrastructure.

The perfect example of the **Iron Law: The Law of Reciprocal Action.**

"What global humanity sows, global humanity shall reap!"

The 13-19th November, 2009, issue of "The Guardian Weekly" headlines:

Crucial data 'distorted' as global oil runs dry.

> "The world is much closer to running out of oil than official estimates admit, according to a whistleblower at the International Energy Agency who claims it has been deliberately underplaying a looming shortage for fear of triggering panic buying.

> The senior official claims the US has played [a significant] role in encouraging the watchdog to underplay the rate of decline while overplaying the chances of finding new reserves.
>
> The allegations raise serious questions about the accuracy of the organisation's latest World Energy Outlook on oil demand and supply to be published this week – which is used by governments around the world to help guide their wider energy and climate change policies."

They go on to say that '...the World Economic Outlook will repeat its previous stance that oil production can be raised from its current level of 83m barrels a day to 105m. However, critics have argued that this cannot be substantiated by firm evidence and say the world has already passed its peak in oil production. Now the 'peak-oil' theory is gaining support at the heart of the global energy establishment. Despite the IEA in 2005 predicting that oil supplies could rise as high as 120m barrels a day by 2030, it was forced to gradually reduce this figure to 116m and then 105m last year, according to the IEA source, who was unwilling to be identified.' He added:

> "The 120m figure always was nonsense but even today's number is much higher than can be justified and the IEA knows this. Many inside the organisation believe that maintaining oil supplies at even 90m to 95m a day would be impossible but there are fears that panic could spread on the financial markets if the figures were brought down further. And the Americans fear the end of oil supremacy because it would threaten their power over access to oil resources."

'A second senior IEA source, who has now left but was also unwilling to give his name, said a key rule at the organisation was that it was "imperative not to anger the Americans" though the fact was that there was not as much oil in the world as had been admitted.' He added: "We have [already] entered the 'peak-oil' zone. I think the situation is really bad."

America also uses vast amounts of another fossil-based commodity to power her industries and economy – coal; once called 'king coal'. Producing around 40 percent of US power generation, coal-fired power stations there produce about 37 percent of carbon emissions. [Source: BBC programme of alternative fuels; January, 2010.]

Who controls and promotes the coal industry in the US? Very large wealthy and powerful Corporates and their equally large numbers of investors who know there is still much money to made from coal generation; never mind the fact that it's contribution to global warming and/or carbon emissions is disproportionate in the extreme.

> "**The West.** *Take the money and run. Do as thou wilt shall be the whole of the Law.* And the drugs internationals and the gambling internationals; ***environmental destruction in the name of progress***; the sexual morality of the mole-rat with attendant plagues; the weapons of mass murder. *And only a few men and women had paused to consider* **that certain behaviour patterns might be wrong.**"
>
> (The Helmet and the Cross. W. H. Canaway. Emphases mine.)

American-style Capitalism, solidly entrenched as the economic model of *choice* for global humanity, now counts among its active adherents former communist foes. Also embracing this now rather 'shaky ideal' are races once under the yoke of colonialism. Two ethnic groups that have benefited financially from various kinds of Treaty or otherwise negotiated 'settlements' are Native Americans; of which some tribes hold considerable wealth from legalised casino operations, and the Maori tribes of New Zealand – also gaining considerable wealth from various 'settlements'.

Given Chief Seattle's clear statement – obviously stemming from the Native American peoples' long association with their environment; the deep spiritual wisdom he elucidates in his address could possibly cause one to wonder whether such peoples would think differently about their new-found tribal wealth. And thus perhaps lead away from the *now-failing* American-style 'Corporate-ethos' into a truly 'spiritualised' economic model which will not go the way of the collapsing *'capitalist money-go-round' carousel.*

Despite the fact that tribal peoples inherently possess an outlook on most issues probably different to their original European colonisers, Dr Elizabeth Rata, a Maori academic at Auckland University, identifies a key aspect of the impact of Capitalism on at least the thinking of current Maori leaders who 'control' this new wealth.

In her perceptive essay: "Retribalisation is all about money", Dr. Rata very succinctly notes:

"...that the tribes have become capitalist corporations through the brokerage of their resources into the national and international economic system. Indeed, corporate groups, such as the new "classed tribe", suit the global order far better than those organisations of individuals who claim economic rights based on democratic principles."

"Tribal-capitalism, along with both western and eastern forms of corporate capitalism, have profound implications for the future of democracy. The essentially pre-democratic nature of corporate capitalism urgently requires exposure and debate."

0.3.5 The Interlinked Global Monetary System: Reaping the Whirlwind! 'A Brief History Lesson.'

The perfect illustration of how **The Law of Reciprocal Action** has impacted on 'human arrogance' can be seen in the almost unbelievable 2008 collapse of once-proud financial institutions right across the globe. There stands perhaps the best 'reality example' of the inviolable nature of this *immutable* Law. It has clearly shown *how* the exercise of human free-will by individuals and groups in the vital 'global financial industry' has wrought carnage for tens of millions. Literally a case of 'sowing the wind' through, quite obviously, free-will greed. Unfortunately for the hundreds of millions who put their faith and finances in the hands of greedy and incompetent 'financial managers'; under the inviolable outworking of the great **Law of Reciprocal Action**, all "reaped the whirlwind". In this case, a Category 5 hurricane.

Note:

This brief history lesson in *this* sub-Segment was originally written for a separate, now-published, Work well before that economic crash in America sent its viral-laden tentacles out to infect the rest of the world. In our increasingly uncertain times, knowledge of **The Spiritual Laws of Creation** readily permits us to 'see' what will come next – *for this is precisely the period of global collapse.*

So: Corporate Capitalism – American style; will we continue to be seduced by you and embrace you more tightly in the belief that your way is the only way? Yes, of course we will. For that is the economic model taught in probably most universities, from which 'Ph.D. toting' economic 'gurus' spew forth to man failing banks and financial houses that yet *still* pressure governments and social paradigms across the globe. Of course, it is not that the *genesis* of the present completely *interlocked system* is American, but was nonetheless perfected there by extremely wealthy men and families of primarily European origin, in concert with the then relatively small but super-wealthy group of home-grown [American] magnates.

> **Note:** The following excerpts and quotes are taken from an early seventies-era book: "**NONE DARE CALL IT CONSPIRACY**". The author, Gary Allen – along with Larry Abraham – had difficulty finding a publisher willing to 'take it on'. (Concord Press. Rossmoor, California.) Once published, however, it became a runaway best-seller in very short order.

- First printing.   February, 1972.   350,000
- Second printing. March, 1972.   1,250,000
- Third printing.   April, 1972.   4,000,000

United States Congressman, **John G. Schmitz**, wrote the following **Introduction** to the work. (Emphases mine.)

> "The story you are about to read is true. The names have not been changed **to protect the guilty**. After reading this book, you will never look at national and world events in the same way again. ...
>
> At first it will receive little publicity and those whose plans are exposed in it will try to kill it by the silent treatment. For reasons that become obvious as you read this book, it will not be reviewed in all the "proper" places or be available on your local bookstand. ...
>
> Having been a college instructor, a State Senator and now a Congressman, I have had experience with real professionals at putting up smokescreens to cover up their own actions **by trying to destroy the accuser**. I hope that you will read this book carefully and draw your own opinions and not accept the opinions of those who of necessity must attempt to discredit the book. **Your future may depend upon it.**"

The many years since 1971 may well have provided data for opponents of the book to offer a different, even recent-historical, perspective. Notwithstanding that 'possibility', what absolutely cannot be refuted in any way whatsoever is the final sentence in John G. Schmitz's **Introduction** to **None Dare Call It Conspiracy.**
i.e. *"Your future may depend upon it."*

Look, now, at what that 'Back to the Future' prediction has wrought for millions of American families alone. Not only have many lost jobs and homes, but whole life-savings have been literally 'wiped out' as well. And from the fall-out, globally, tens of millions jobless.

Gary Allen notes that American President **F.D.R.** once said:

> "In politics, nothing happens by accident. If it happens, you can bet it was planned that way."

The whole of human history clearly attests to the fact that through exercising our inherent, free-will attribute, we *humans* engineer human events and outcomes. Decisions must *always* produce consequences – or 'outcomes'! Thus the unseen yet nonetheless immutable 'driving power' of **"The Law Of Reciprocal Action"**.

Gary Allen tells us that decades ago Professor Carroll Quigley, who taught at the Foreign Service School in Georgetown University and also at Princeton and Harvard, produced a 1300 page, 8 pound tome – *Tragedy and Hope* – detailing exactly the process by which the world became economically interlocked, **and who engineered it.** Thus the **How** and the **Why!** The **Why** is simple enough: Professor Quigley states it as:

> "...nothing less than to create a world system of financial control in private hands able to dominate the political system of each country and the economy of the world as a whole."

The **How**, however, is the stuff of conspiracy; of which we all must disbelieve and mock or be labelled silly conspiracy-theorists. Yet Montagu Norman, a former head of the Bank of England, stated:

> "...that the Hegemony of World Finance should reign supreme over everyone, everywhere, as one whole *supernational control mechanism.*"

To that conspiratorial end, the author, on page 9, very early on asks a key question. [Emphasis mine.]

> "Why is it that virtually all 'reputable' scholars and mass media columnists and commentators reject the cause and effect or conspiratorial theory of history? Primarily, most scholars *follow the crowd* in the academic world just as most women follow fashions. To buck the tide means social and professional ostracism. The same is true of the mass media."

So despite the fact that 'lone voices' are often labelled 'conspiracy theorists', the history that Professor Quigley details is exactly that – the *history* of *how* the *world* financial system became *interlocked.*

Perhaps the most interesting aspect of the 2008 financial crunch which began in the U.S.A. is the fact that the American Constitution – a defining humanitarian document by any standard – espouses certain freedoms and inalienable rights written into it by America's Founding Fathers. Yet despite the sacrosanct nature of that document, certain of those 'rights' have nonetheless been *subverted* by 'modern legal machinations' in the U.S. The same kind of 'activity' can now be clearly seen to have occurred in the subversion of the financial system by powerful and greedy individuals and self-interest groups.

Gary Allen noted that: 'The architects of The American Constitution revolted against the near-total government of the English Monarchy. Knowing that having no government at all would lead to chaos, they set up a Constitutional Republic with a very limited government.' Thomas Jefferson said:

> "In questions of power then let no more be heard of confidence in man, but bind him down from mischief by the chains of the Constitution."

Allen writes that Jefferson knew that if the government were not enslaved, people soon would be, so the Constitution *fractionalised* and *subdivided* governmental power in every way possible. Under such a system no segment of government could amass enough [political] power to form a dictatorship.

Financial power – and thus control – is far more potent, however, and America's Founding Fathers certainly understood that reality. Wealthy European bankers had long perfected the technique of bank/wealth consolidation, and through key men of those banking houses migrated the same ideas to the "New World". The Bank of England, Bank of France and Bank of Germany were not owned by their respective governments, but were privately owned monopolies granted by the heads of state, usually in return for loans. Under this system, Reginald Mckenna, President of the Midlands Bank of England, observed:

> "Those that issue the money and credit direct the policies of government and hold in their hands the destiny of the people."

From the earliest days, the Founding Fathers had been conscious of attempts to control America through money manipulation, and they carried on a running battle with the international bankers. Thomas Jefferson wrote to John Adams:

> "...I sincerely believe, with you, that banking establishments are more dangerous than standing armies..."

From a very early time in American history, banks were primarily independent entities and often individually-owned, set up to serve a need: e.g.; as brokers in the early fur trade. So in the 'cow-towns' and mining towns of a rapidly-growing 19th century America, these independently-owned banks sprang up to service the increasingly sophisticated, permanent towns 'across the frontier'.

However, individually-owned banks did not suit the aims and goals of the European bankers then becoming firmly established in the key cities of the east. Plans were formulated to bring all banks under a single controlling umbrella. But how to achieve it and make it stick? Create artificial panic. Senator Robert Owen, a co-author of the Federal Reserve Act, (who later deeply regretted his role), testified before a Congressional Committee that the bank he owned received from the National Bankers Association what came to be known as the "Panic Circular of 1893". It stated:

> "You will retire one-third of your circulation and call in one-half of your loans..."

The next 'panic', in the autumn of 1907, was precipitated by the American banking tycoon, J.P. Morgan. Historian Frederick Lewis Allen tells in *Life* magazine of April 25th, 1949, of Morgan's role in spreading rumours of insolvency of the Knickerbocker bank and The Trust Company of America, which rumours triggered the 1907 panic.

> "Oakleigh Thorne, the president of that particular trust company, testified later before a congressional committee that his bank had been subjected to only moderate withdrawals ...[and that Morgan's machinations] ... had caused the run on his bank. From this testimony, plus the disciplinary measures taken by the Clearing House against the Heinze, Morse and Thomas banks, plus other fragments of supposedly pertinent evidence, certain chroniclers have arrived at the ingenious conclusion that the Morgan interests took advantage of the unsettled conditions during the autumn of 1907 to precipitate the panic, guiding it shrewdly as it progressed so that it would kill off rival banks and consolidate the pre-eminence of the banks within the Morgan orbit."

Frederick Lewis went on to explain that the "panic" which Morgan had created, he proceeded to end almost single-handedly. He had made his point.

> "The lesson of the panic of 1907 was clear, though not for some six years was it destined to be embodied in legislation: the United States gravely needed a central banking system..."

After the Panic of 1907, Senator Aldrich, even though having no technical knowledge of banking, was appointed to head the National Monetary Commission by fellow Senators. A tour to Europe, courtesy of American taxpayers, quickly followed. There, wined and dined by the owners of Europe's central banks, they 'studied' central banking. No meetings were held and no reports were made for two years. Aldrich, along with Paul Warburg and other international bankers, staged one of the most important secret meetings in the history of the United States. Rockefeller agent Frank Vanderlip admitted many years later in his memoirs:

> "Despite my views about the value to society of greater publicity for the affairs of corporations, there was an occasion, near the close of 1910, when I was as secretive – indeed as furtive – as any conspirator .... I do not feel it as any exaggeration to speak of our secret expedition to Jekyl Island as the occasion of the actual conception of what eventually became the Federal Reserve System." (p.46)

Gary Allen writes that the secrecy was well warranted, for at stake was control over the entire economy. 'At Jekyl Island, B.C. Forbes in his *Men Who Are Making America*, notes':

> "After a general discussion it was decided to draw up certain broad principles on which all could agree. Every member of the group voted for a central bank as being the ideal cornerstone for any banking system." (Page 399)

It is interesting to also note here the following points:

- Warburg stressed that the name "central bank" be avoided at all costs. Instead, it was decided to promote the scheme as a "regional reserve" system with four (later twelve) branches in different sections of the country.
- Out of the Jekyl Island meeting came the completion of the Monetary Commission Report and the Aldrich Bill.
- Warburg proposed that the bill be designated the "Federal Reserve System" but Aldrich insisted his own name was already associated in the public's mind with banking reform and that it would arouse suspicion if a bill were introduced which did *not* bear his name.
- So strong was public opposition to such reform that Aldrich's name attached to the bill proved to be the kiss of death, since any law bearing his name was so obviously a project of the international bankers.
- Because the Aldrich Bill could not be pushed through, a new strategy was devised.

The Federal Reserve Act was passed on December 22nd, 1913, by a large majority in the House, but a narrower margin in the Senate. There *was* genuine opposition to the Act, but it could not match the power of the bill's advocates. Conservative Henry Cabot Lodge Sr. proclaimed with great foresight:

> "The bill as it stands seems to me to open the way to a vast inflation of currency ... I do not like to think that any law can be passed which will make it possible to submerge the gold standard in *a flood of irredeemable paper currency.*"
> (*Congressional Record*, June 10th, 1932. [Italics mine.])

After the vote, Congressman Charles A. Lindbergh Sr., father of the famous aviator, told Congress:

> "This act establishes the most gigantic trust on earth. ...When the President signs this act the invisible government by the money power, proven to exist by the Money Trust investigation, will be legalized. ... ...
> The new law will create inflation whenever the trusts want inflation. ..."

How powerful is the "central bank" of America? The Federal Reserve controls [our] money supply and interest rates, and thereby manipulates the entire economy – creating inflation or deflation, recession or boom, and sending the stock markets up or down at whim. The Federal Reserve is so powerful that Congressman Wright Patterson, chairman of the House Banking Committee, [maintains]:

> "In the United States today we have in effect two governments. ... We have the duly constituted Government. ... Then we have an independent, uncontrolled and uncoordinated government in the Federal Reserve System, operating the money powers *which are reserved to Congress by the Constitution*." (Emphasis mine.)

Allen notes that 'neither Presidents, Congressmen nor Secretaries of the Treasury direct the Federal Reserve! In the matters of money, the Federal Reserve directs them. The uncontrolled power of the "Fed" was admitted by Secretary of the Treasury David M. Kennedy in an interview back in 1969 for the May issue of *U.S. News and World Report*'.[8]

> Q. "Do you approve of the latest credit-tightening moves?"
> A. "It's not my job to approve or disapprove. It is the action of the Federal Reserve."

Allen writes that 'the members of the Federal Reserve Board [are] appointed by the President for fourteen year terms. Since these positions control the entire economy of the country they are far more important than cabinet positions...' (p.56)

Prior to the actual day of the crash of 1929, Paul Warburg, one of the architects of the Federal Reserve Act, provided the warning to sell. That signal came on March 9 of that year when the Financial Chronicle quoted Warburg as giving this sound advice:

> "If orgies of unrestricted speculation are permitted to spread too far ... the ultimate collapse is certain ... to bring about a general depression involving the whole country."
> The author says: 'To think that the scientifically engineered Crash of '29 was an accident or the result of stupidity defies all logic. The international bankers who promoted the inflationary policies and pushed the propaganda which pumped

---

[8]The history of the 'Fed' may be viewed online at www.docu-view.com ["History of the Federal Reserve (money wasters.)]

up the stock market represented too many generations of accumulated expertise to have blundered into "the great depression".'

Can we state "the collapse of 2008" to be a depression? Not according to the 'experts'. It tends only *toward* a recession they say, never mind the fact that factory closures are the result, along with millions out of work globally. It is said that 'when America coughs, the world sneezes'. Since "The Great Depression" there have been regular recessions.

Gary Allen notes that: 'Each of these has followed a period in which the Federal Reserve tromped down hard on the money accelerator and then slammed on the brakes. Since 1929 the following recessions have been created by such manipulation.'

- 1936–1937   Stock Prices fell fifty percent.
- 1948   Stock prices dropped sixteen percent.
- 1953   Stock declined thirteen percent.
- 1956–1957   The market dipped thirteen percent.
- 1957   The same year, a drop of nineteen percent.
- 1960   The market was off seventeen percent.
- 1966   Stock prices plummeted twenty-five percent.
- 1970   The market plunged over twenty-five percent.

Since then we have had the "oil-shock" crisis of 1973, and regular downturns in the 80's, 90's and the first decade of the new century to the definitive "crash" of 2008. So either it is all manipulated by very wealthy 'insiders' to increase their wealth markedly, or the so-called economic gurus are not expert at all – despite their much-lauded university qualifications. We should not forget that in the West at least, the media outlets of newspapers and TV etc., are primarily controlled by just a few super-wealthy tycoons and their families. So any suggestion of conspiratorial financial or share-market manipulation by the same 'super-wealthy' can easily be shut down through public ridicule and/or disinformation.

Despite the latest 'crash' bringing about the free-fall of global stocks and swallowing up banks and billions of dollars to simply disappear into an 'invisible vortex' somewhere, governments and the larger international banks were still able to find the mind-boggling tens of billions to prop up the tottering, inter-connected edifice from total global collapse. Now the *country* of America is in debt to the tune of *trillions* of dollars. Much of America is not owned by Americans at all but by foreign guarantors of multi-billion dollar loans to help keep all things American at least 'above water'.

From the Federal Reserve Bank later came the notion and reality of the World Bank, and then, later still, the International Monetary Fund. Three powerful financial entities with massive and *historically-unprecedented* global control. Akin to The Three Musketeers mantra: **"All for One – One for All!"** – *all* felt the crunch together.

That is not the end of it by any means, however. No! When the *final* collapse does arrive, it will not be **The Three Musketeers** then who might rescue each other. For the managerial practices of obscenely rewarded 'financial experts' – like those who ran the ridiculously, but *appropriately*, named "Freddy Mac" and "Fanny Mae" entities – will finally be understood to have been similar to the antics of **"The Three Stooges"**. Unfortunately, however, without the humour; just the suffering – for millions!

Yet the buzz-word of the 'big three' at this time is still Globalisation; the concerted target of angry, alienated and galvanised peoples from all nationalities and all walks of life. Money is power in this rotten, insidiously-evil, inequitable world **we humans have created**. Latter-day Chinese economic 'pressure' in the guise of aid in Africa and the Pacific have seen countries subvert part of *their* control and perhaps sovereignty to the controlling-power of money. China is the new emerging economic superpower, to which most countries kow-tow for free-trade deals. At least that was the position before the 2008 global collapse closed factories and sent Chinese workers scurrying back to the hinterland.

Do we think that this small history lesson is necessary? Or should we continue on as before?

Perhaps we should take serious note of Einstein's marvellous definition of senility:

> **"To keep on doing the same things and expect different results."**

By virtue of Einstein's wonderfully-logical insight here, along with certain historical realities, it would be foolish to believe that the current kinds of 'rescue packages' that have been applied to the global financial crisis by various governments will *once and for all* finally cure a 'very sick system'. Quite clearly, the 'same-old' will simply repeat the 'same-old'. We should therefore take serious note of this short history lesson, for 'what has gone before' ***will replay again***; and probably sooner rather than later, *if* – as **George Soros** has long-tried to warn – there is *no change in the system itself.*

From science: **"For every action, there is an equal and opposite reaction!"**

From the more decisive power inherent in **Spiritual Law**: "What **Global Humanity Sows,**
Global Humanity Shall Reap."
In this case, however, precisely because of the tightly-linked global monetary system – to which the Nations of the world have *voluntarily surrendered* their financial sovereignty – the associated "reaping" was seeded by a relatively few. Therefore:
"What 'financial experts' *sowed*, **the 'whole world'** *reaped.*"

Conceived in Wall Street, the mantra, "**Greed is good**", became the ethos of 'financial gurus' worldwide before the global bonfire turned to ash what effectively was a massive pile of 'irredeemable paper currency'. Greed: Certainly not one of the spiritual virtues humankind is seriously enjoined to live by. Glaringly-obviously, an opposite kind of ethos *would not* have brought the spectacular financial meltdown that occurred. In 2009 the currency speculators were trading again. No curbs have been placed on such practices by the *new regulators*, yet these *manipulators* produce *nothing* of value. All seek personal wealth only.

As we all now dramatically understand from the hard lesson of 2008, the **'reaction'**; the **'reaping'**, is far more dire than any *standard* prediction could possibly have foreseen. Thus can we observe the Truth of **Creation-Law**:
That the 'reaction/reaping/outcome' from every/all originating decision/s *must always be greater **in the 'return'.*** If we were to state that fact ten million times, and say it *yet again*; it could *never change* in its *immutable* and *inviolable* outworking.

Director Michael Moore, much maligned by some but nonetheless possessing the requisite courage to document shocking realities about life and Law in "the land of the free"; in his key movie – "**Capitalism. A Love Story**" – exposes the hypocritical and callous greed of America's 'money-men'. Deriving from that very 'mind-set'; the subsequent collapse of industries and the social disruption and dislocation of a huge segment of American society.

Perhaps to add "insult to injury"; Gerald Celente, CEO of Trends Research Institute who predicted the 1987 stock market crash and the fall of the Soviet Union, says that by 2012 'America will become an undeveloped Nation'. "Food riots, squatter rebellions [documented by Michael Moore], tax revolts and job marches" will characterise the 'revolution'.

> "We're going to start seeing huge areas of vacant real estate and squatters living in them .... Its going to be a picture the likes of which Americans are not ... used to. Its going to come as a shock and with it, ... a lot of crime. [That] is going to be a lot worse than it was before because in the last 1929 Depression, people's minds weren't wrecked on all these modern drugs – over-the-counter drugs, or crystal meth or whatever it might be. So, you have a huge underclass of very desperate people with their minds chemically blown beyond anybody's comprehension."

The predictive accuracy of Gerald Celente and Trends Research Institute is vouched for by prestigious American institutions such as CNN, USA Today, CNBC, The Atlanta Journal-Constitution, The New York Times, 48 Hours/CBS News, The Detroit News, The Los Angeles Times and The New York Post. And, in perhaps a truly mad twist, The Wall Street Journal.

There is no doubt that America *will* collapse. For despite the strong ethos of Calvinism *and* "**Manifest Destiny**" that defined early settlement, that 'pairing' failed to *permanently anchor* the *right* governmental and societal moral and ethical foundation in the country. So what we now witness for America and its people is nothing more than the inevitable 'reaping' from the 'sowing' of two *solidly-entrenched* aspects of the *American ethos*.

One is the disturbing, sometimes terrible, at times evil, decision-making on the part of certain branches of successive American Administrations, particularly since the late 1950's. For no country can promote itself as a God-fearing and obedient Nation *ostensibly* embracing the associated Higher Laws that must come with such a stance and then hypocritically continually transgress those very Laws without there being serious repercussions for ***all*** in the land. For ***all*** have taken part in the democratic processes that have brought forth the politicians who enact *human* laws which *always oppose* the **Higher Immutable**, thus **Inviolable, Creation-Law**.

The second is the almost *rabid* promotion across the globe of American-style Capitalism, which has revealed itself to be a two-edged sword – *as it would*. Even though very much a Communist State, China's enthusiastic embracing of so-called *clever* American business 'know-how' has not only threatened industry in America, but in many other countries globally. Now that China has recovered from the 2008 'collapse' and is once again in a high-growth mind-set, there is the very real possibility that if the trend continues *without interruption*, China will soon wrest from America the dubious and totally *aspiritual* title as 'the world's only superpower'.

In *human* history, the ***legacy*** of the rise and ***fall*** of ***all*** the 'great' empires has resulted in the world we know today. If we follow, *chronologically*, the time-line of the emergence, life and collapse of all previous 'empires', we can observe a most interesting *broad-sweep aspect* therein. It is one which basically notes that the ***closer*** to our present time particular 'empires' flourished, the ***shorter*** their ***life-span*** – particularly from the 19th century.

Now the *last* two 'empires' that will ever exist on earth overlap in tandem. Though both regimes would 'diplomatically' deny it, both are nonetheless vying for global supremacy, militarily and economically. Militarily the most powerful country to have ever existed, the U.S.A. is nonetheless on the wane. The rapid rise of the U.S. – primarily in the 20th century – and China's spectacular and escalating ascendency in the first decade of the 21st century coincides in real time to vastly increasing ***spiritual power and pressure*** driving literally *everything* to its final point of either *upliftment* – or *total collapse*.

Our "waning empire", the U.S.A., ostensibly holds **The Creator** and **His Laws** as its core ethos, yet lives a sham life. Our "ascending empire", China, on the other hand views its past and its future destiny as being inextricably intertwined with "the ancestors" – thus holding to the "spiritually-dead" ethos of "ancestor worship". So both must, and will, fall!

As we stressed early on in this Booklet: "*Without Revelation a Nation fades.* **But it prospers by knowing The Law**."

Thus **the good** – *that which adjusts itself to The Laws* – **will prosper**. And **the bad or wrong** – *that which opposes The Laws*

– **will collapse**. In this simple equation resides an infallible standard by which to measure events around us and to choose accordingly.

The nightly news images of "**Global Societal Collapse**" bear immutable witness to this *unstoppable* force.

Greed is good! Therefore consumption must be good, for consumption means greater profits for Corporations and their shareholders – and China. By extension, Capitalism must also be good, for that is the mechanism which brought it all into being and allows it to continue. Even though it can surely be seen that it is unsustainable in its present form, the mad carousel of Capitalism – which no one person or organisation [apart from George Soros apparently] has the courage to call for an end to and institute a different mechanism for trade etc., – continues to steadily and inexorably fail.

The world runs on hypocrisy! Whether it be in economics, politics, religion, or focussed on cultural, ethnic and racial 'priorities'; all say one thing – but do another. And all would deny doing such a thing. Such is the way of the shrewdly-calculating human intellect; totally devoid of ***truly genuine*** spiritual aspirations.

An example; the great ecological disaster of 2010 – the Gulf of Mexico oil leak. Finger-pointing and blame – at weak Government legislation, at Corporate oil-giant greed and shoddy operational short-cut practices etc., – cannot mask the reality that irrespective of who or what was to blame, the resultant outcome shows the *immutable outworking* of the great and inviolable **Law of Reciprocal Action: What we sow we [MUST] reap!**

An overly-affluent society that based the greater part of its economy and wealth on oil; that has long-consumed far more than it had a moral right to, now struggles to understand how such a disaster could have occurred.

An alternative view states that allowing millions of litres of crude to spill for months, thereby destroying part of the fishing industry, would help the U.S. Govt. to open more of the Gulf to more oil exploration. The standard chemical used to sink and disperse the crude oil is known to be ten times more toxic than crude itself, thus devastating marine life. Since 'home-grown' oil lessens dependency on foreign oil, the U.S. Govt. has now opened virtually all of the Gulf to exploration.

In the aftermath of the financial bonfire of 2008, President Obama issued new directives to change the 'system' so as to prevent any future repeat of the meltdown. He blamed the financial crisis on "a culture of irresponsibility". Commenting on the billions of dollars lost through 'a record [number] of mortgage foreclosures ... on mortgage loans and securities backed by subprime mortgages', he said: — "It was easy money. But these schemes were built on a pile of sand."

The Obama plan gave new powers to the Federal Reserve to oversee the entire financial system. It is hoped that the central bank will be able to deal with the kinds of problems that were allowed to build to such an extent that they finally overwhelmed America's financial system in the spectacular "Bonfire of the Billionaires".

It was a 'bonfire' so life-changing that a few of the world's super-rich, because of their losses, amazingly even committed suicide; never mind the fact that those particular individuals still had billions left to play with. Surely the perfect illustration of the great Spiritual Truth:

"What does it profit a man if he gains the whole world, but loses his soul." And from Luke; a warning from the past for today. [Fenton, 21:34-36]

> "But take care of yourselves, for fear your hearts should be loaded with debauchery, and drunkenness, **and business cares**, and that day come swiftly upon you like a snare; for thus it will come upon all dwelling upon the face of the earth. Watch, therefore, at every season, offering prayer; so that you may be prepared to escape **all the coming calamities**..."

Surely here is the greatest warning yet to the corporate world and its financiers, exchange-rate manipulators, share-market fanatics and all of similar ilk who elevate the *god-corporate* and the *god-financial* before all else.

Will President Obama's plan work? Only time will tell, of course. However, two years after the great crash, 2010 saw European governments struggling to cope with *new* levels of high debt. And 2011 not only sees that trend worsening, but also the curious fact that none of the *real* Wall St. villains have yet been called to account.

One sure way in which the capitalist greed generated from Wall St. would be eliminated forever would be for 'Mother Nature' to bring forth for the U.S. two possible nightmarish scenarios, both already primed and waiting. "She", after all – **with her truly wondrous power** – is the best "lawful" destroyer of man's works and societal infrastructure, and Governments *know* they could never really cope with a real *super* natural disaster. For it **is** given over to the **"Forces of Nature"** to finally bring to an end humankind's so-long-standing – and still ongoing – foolish and totally intransigent opposition to the very Laws and Rules set into Creation which we were to obey, that we might know *genuine* peace and harmony.

The great eighth century Prophet, Isaiah [24:4-6], succinctly encapsulated in just **one sentence** *exactly* what it was that we *should* have obeyed – **but did not**. That single sentence/prophecy – *which we must reinforce often* – provides the very **why** for the societal horrors now upon us, never mind the *far greater* global angst awaiting its time of *full impact*.

> 'The "Earth" also is defiled under the inhabitants thereof;
> because they have
> <u>*transgressed*</u> the "Laws",
> <u>*changed*</u> the decrees,
> <u>*broken*</u> the everlasting covenant.'

How many times do we have to be warned? The outcome for our unbelievable arrogance...? The great Prophet does not mince words.

"Therefore has the curse devoured the "Earth", **and those that dwell therein are desolate**:..."

Reported in *The Economist* in January 2005
– <u>**UN Warns of Apocalypse Now**</u> –
UN emergency relief director Jan Egeland painted an apocalyptic picture.

'Earthquakes, floods and other natural disasters could kill millions in the world's mega-cities and time is running out to prevent such catastrophes, the United Nations warns. Mega-cities have 10 million or more people, many concentrated in slums.'

"Perhaps the most frightening prospect would be to have a truly mega-disaster in a mega-city," Egeland told the World Disaster Prevention Conference. "Then we could have not only a tsunami-style casualty rate as we saw on Boxing Day, but one that's one hundred times that." He said "time is running out" to prevent such a catastrophe.

The greater Tokyo area, with a population of more than 35 million, tops the list of mega-cities, followed by Mexico City at

19 million, greater New York at 18.5 million and Bombay at 18.3 million.'

One apocalyptic scenario for the U.S. is the supervolcano in Yellowstone, *'due'* to blow again. The Yellowstone caldera would discharge so much material that American society would be reduced to Third-world status in very short order. The impact from the same material would also be disastrous globally. From Matthew 24:19-22, Fenton:

> "...Pray, however, that your flight may not come during the winter, nor upon a Rest-day; for there shall **then** be widespread affliction, such as has **not been known since the beginning of the world until now**, no, nor will *ever* be known again...."

The second *destroyer* for the U.S. could well be the *active* Mt. Cumbrevieja volcano in the Canary Islands. If it were to erupt and fulfil the absolute *worst-case* scenario, the result would be a true *mega-tsunami* impacting the Eastern seaboard of the Americas' from Newfoundland to Central America, with the major hit on the U.S. Travelling at a speed of 720 km per hour, it would take just 8 hours to cross the Atlantic and destroy all cities and infrastructure along that coastline. [Question: Could the Yellowstone supervolcano eruption in its turn also trigger a Mt. Cumbrevieja eruption? A frightening scenario for the U.S.]

Some scientists estimate that the wave *could* reach as high as **500 metres at impact.** Such a wave would easily destroy not only the cities along the East Coast, but would reach many miles inland via the large rivers that flow into the Atlantic. Devastation would virtually be complete, and financial and infrastructural recovery might well be impossible. Mt. Cumbrevieja, too, could reduce the U.S. to Third-world status. Wall St., however, would be effaced from the earth.

> "And there will be signs in the sun, and moon, and stars; and upon the earth nations in despair, as when in terror of **the roaring and raging sea**; men expiring from fear, and apprehension of what is coming upon the world:..."

(Luke 21:25-26, Fenton.)

So: If we take the one stark and irrefutable fact that emerges from the 2008 financial 'experience'; it is:

"That the 2008 virtual collapse of the global money markets clearly reveal that its *foundation* was wrong. For it was founded just on human ideas and greed, **not** on the knowledge of **Creation-Law**. So to continue with policies that have proven time and time again to not only be problematic but to cause suffering and social distress to the many whilst insulating the *super-wealthy*, eventually guarantees a completely-irretrievable, total and utter collapse. Only then, however, can a new and ***spiritually-equitable*** financial and trade foundation finally be established."

(Author.)

So is The Law written! So shall it one day be!

<u>America</u>: How far your <u>spiritual fall</u> since your moral high point and great blood-sacrifice in The Second World War, and your noble generosity toward others immediately following that terrible era! How much must you <u>yet reap</u> through the Immutable outworking of "<u>**CREATION-LAW**</u>"; let alone your appalling 'legal' distortions of just the 1st and 2nd Amendments – on their own – of your <u>once-ennobled</u> Founding Constitution?

0.4 The Law of Attraction of Similar Species!

0.4.1 Like Attracts Like.

This Law, in its correct form as **The Law of Attraction of Similar Species**, is aptly expressed in sayings such as, "Birds of a feather flock together". How strongly mankind even unconsciously lives this particular Law is illustrated in another saying: "You can tell a man by the company he keeps". In essence, we constantly live this Law at the everyday social and work level even though we may not be aware of it or its far-reaching implications. Yet its effects can be readily observed around us every single day. Like-minded people gravitate toward certain occupations and professions. In our recreational time the same factors apply. A more striking example, however, may be found at large social gatherings where small groups will form themselves based on what they have in common. It may be their religion or spiritual beliefs, political leanings, profession, musical tastes, sports, language or race, a particular love of something, or even a shared hatred. It can be any number of things or varying combinations, but it will always be a reflection of "The Law of Attraction..." in operation.

Some ancient peoples were aware of the effect of this important Law and followed it unconsciously in that they separated out into occupational and educational classes, crafts and Guilds. In that spiritually correct system, every member of society had the opportunity to live and develop to his fullest potential within each particular "level" attained to. Unfortunately societies gradually changed into divisions of upper, middle and lower classes. This development eventually embraced the full social spectrum of envy and hatred on the one hand, and conceit and arrogance on the other, until finally ending in class-conflict.

What is infinitely more beneficial, and clearly desirable, is that the various occupations and socio-economic groups in societies develop in such a way that they stand "side by side", thus offering the greatest possibility for "working together" harmoniously. Genuine self-esteem for every group could develop to its fullest potential then. And because the different sectors will possess abilities that the others might not have, each becomes a necessary link to every other, thus producing a sound whole. Anti-social problems should then gradually disappear as a better society develops under the correct recognition of this Law. The key consideration here, however, is: *"Working Together, Side by Side!"*

In a completely different kind of example, gardening can show the extent of this Law quite graphically. In the practice of "companion-planting", one type of plant or group of plants assists the growth and development of others. An "inappropriate" plant, however, can actually prevent the "companion" from reaching full maturity or producing fruit. In the wild communities of plants this "Law of Attraction..." guarantees a natural balance of the various groupings. With the exception of a few species, the animal world operates under the same principle, as do the birds and fishes. The advantages of groupings are quite obvious, a greater protective umbrella and care of the offspring probably being the primary consideration. In working together, food supplies may be more secure and the group entity is better able to develop a higher social structure than lone individuals can.

"The Law of Attraction..." also guarantees that if a particular species is split, the split parts will seek to re-unite when given the opportunity. In terms of the attracting quality, whole species that are similar will attract, and split parts of the same species will also strive to re-unite. This Law is a fundamental necessity for everything seeking union in Creation.

What does this mean for us, the human species? And where do we place this powerful force of attraction between men and women? Because of its nature and place in Creation, the human being also carries, as an inherent quality within it, the desire for union. Sexual instinct aside, this basically explains the natural attraction between man and woman.

As previously stated, we possess the ability, by virtue of our spiritual nature, to produce the forms of our thoughts, words and deeds. What has not been stated, however, is the fact that these forms, which are our *works*, are *whole species*. Therefore, under the outworking of this particular Law they, in turn, attract *similar species*. Since man is unable to *stop forming*, what, then, do we have? What are thereby produced are extremely large groupings of correspondingly *similar* forms to the *particular kinds of thoughts generated*. These homogeneous groupings we can designate as "power centres".

This is an apt description as they *do* possess power. By employing the power inherent in our everyday thought-processes we not only produced them in the first place, but automatically sustain – and thus maintain – all the many and varied "centres" now in existence: the dark, dangerous and evil, and the light, good and beneficial. And depending on our personal nature and volition, we therewith automatically connect to those with which we will have a respective affinity. We can, moreover, greatly increase the size and power of these "centres" by "feeding" them *greatly intensified* thoughts, particularly those of hate, envy and anger etc..

Where, then, do these "power centres" reside, and what is their function? They exist in their non-material state close to our physical environment. From there they are easily able to influence the affairs of men – *if men **choose** to attach themselves to*, and therefore *extract substance from*, the particular "power centre/s" of their choice. That is, the one/s exactly corresponding to the nature of the thoughts at any given time. For each "centre" corresponds with, and attracts to itself, the *same kinds* of similar forms. Thus there are "power centres" of all the virtues and vices from the "works" of humankind. Simple use of our imagination can offer an indication of how some might look. Those of hate, jealousy and bitterness must be ugly to witness, whilst those of love and kindness would be havens of happiness and peace. A small illustration of how The Spiritual Laws intermesh and how the effect of these "power centres" on human beings can be so terribly devastating

– even if the recipient has absolutely no knowledge whatsoever of them – can reveal how insidiously powerful they are.

We have now learned that ignorance of The Laws does not *prevent* the dispensing of true justice. Marriage and the family unit, by virtue of the closeness of the relationships, is invariably a place where much emotion – both beneficial and unhelpful – is generated. So, should a situation develop where a breaking down of what might once have been a relatively happy unit degenerates into a difficult and perhaps bitter experience for one or both partners, the emotional pain will produce forms associated with that turmoil.

This will probably be compounded if there is a third party involved and/or there are children to the marriage. If there can be no reconciliation or resolution and a breakdown is inevitable, the emotional pressures generated might be such that the normal strength of one of the partners is temporarily rendered far weaker than would otherwise be the case. With the ebbing of "spiritual strength" – this "strength" being at the same time also spiritual protection – in the belief that one's hopes and dreams are about to be dashed, there may arise in the mind of *the one most likely to suffer the greatest loss*, the wish to "do something about it". More particularly with the possible estrangement from everyday contact with much loved children.

This potential chain of events may only begin as just the emotion of hurt and then perhaps anger. If it stays at that level and is resolved relatively peacefully, nothing untoward should occur to bring about a dangerous situation. However, should it develop further to the point of one partner "wanting to get even", the forms generated by the powerful emotions of such a situation – i.e., those of hate and revenge – begin the process of attracting around that individual correspondingly similar forms from the relevant "power centre/s".

His developing volition for revenge is thus *strengthened* to a considerable degree under this "Law of Attraction of Similar Species". If the individual cannot then generate sufficient spiritual strength to resist a rapidly weakening *former good volition*, and thus *change the forms around him*, it could well be that at the moment of greatest weakness, the pressure from the "attacking" similar forms "forces" the carrying out of a tragic deed.

How often do we hear comments evinced with great puzzlement: "How could he/she have done that?" "It is so totally out of character!" "I would never have believed that he/she could ever be capable of doing that!" Ordinarily, it would probably never have happened. However, with the base volition at such a time vastly amplified by the other attracted forms, the receiver is rendered temporarily incapable of clear and logical reasoning. Other "forces" have "taken over". That lawful process offers a good explanation of the Biblical Scripture:

> "Because our fight is **not** against blood and flesh; but against the sovereignties, against the powers, against the commanders of the darkness of this world..."
>
> (Ephesians 6:12, Fenton.)

Unfortunately, however, it is a darkness that humankind has created. With the exception of true insanity – and/or in cases where the personal free-will volition of a person is temporarily rendered impotent by a stronger *occupying entity* – the perpetrator is, nonetheless, still spiritually responsible for his actions. Therefore, irrespective of the circumstances – or even possible provocation – it still rests with the individual whether or not he chooses a good volition or a dark one. It should never be forgotten that we are always subject to *the whirlwind constant*. We may believe we are only *sowing the wind* but, under Spiritual Law, we **will** *reap the whirlwind*. The harvesting must always be greater than the sowing and this is equally true in good or bad. Neither can we escape the effects of our works at earthly death.

The following Bible Scripture states it succinctly:

> "...and their works accompany them"
>
> (Revelation 14:13, Fenton.)

Consequently, no one can escape Spiritual Justice purely because one conveniently dies an earthly death. No, the "works" spoken of here are composed of **all the forms** produced by our thoughts, our words, and our actions or deeds. Because we are the producers, the originators, of them, they are tied to us until such time as we finally undertake to expiate them, either upon their return to us as possible hard lessons or experiences, or we bring about a change in the nature of them by a corresponding change in our own personal attitude and spiritual volition. Thus, in strict accordance with The Laws of Justice, *what has not been dealt with and completely expiated on the earth* waits to be faced in the planes of what we loosely refer to as "the beyond". For we **cannot** escape "our works". *They follow us, purely and simply because they must – **because they are ours**.*

The birth of Jesus into the Jewish race provides an excellent example of how "The Law of Attraction..." operates in its inviolable way. As a people with strong religious convictions, the Israelites through their prophets divined the existence of The One Invisible God thus anchoring a channel of *knowing acceptance* of, and for, messages and events from that Highest Source. The strength of this exalted belief, even in times of hard persecution, was such that it reached upward to the Godhead Itself thus permitting the strongest possible *spiritual* connection to It at that time. The Jewish people, therefore, were able to provide the necessary "spiritual connection" for the birth of Jesus to take place. Hence the reason why Jesus, the Son of the Invisible God **could**, and **did**, incarnate into that particular race.

For only with such a sure conviction from the Jewish people could the appropriate connections be established for such an event to take place. Without this inner divining of the "Highest Heights", a necessary attracting quality for this happening was impossible. An incarnation by Jesus into any race other than one with the requisite spiritual belief of the Highest Spheres would mean a huge gulf of non-understanding, so is not possible under The Laws of Creation. Quite logically, therefore, an incarnation into a savage tribe of idol worshippers would have been a rather pointless exercise for the entry of the Son of God onto the Earth Plane.

0.4.2 Spiritual Qualities as the First Consideration.

Because we are inherently imbued with the nature and quality of The Spiritual, the potential to develop the correspondingly more ennobled characteristics *should* be the primary factor that determines to whom or to what we will be naturally attracted. Most people will have probably felt strongly drawn to certain persons for no *apparent* reason other than a feeling of an especially strong bond. Sometimes to our great surprise - though it should not be so under the effect of the "Law of Attraction..." - we may even discover that certain meetings quickly produce bonds that are far stronger than those we experience with some members of our own immediate family.

As previously alluded to earlier in this Booklet, a particular story in the life of Jesus illustrates this fact perfectly. When told that His mother and brothers were waiting to see Him, replied:

> "Who is My mother? and who are My brothers?" Then extending His hand in the direction of His disciples, He said, "Why, those are My mother and My brothers! For whosoever does the will of My Father Who is in Heaven, he is My brother, and sister, and mother!
>
> (Matthew 12:48-50, Fenton.)

Spiritual qualities, therefore, should be recognised as the correct thing to strive for in the first instance, even if it means breaking free from the sometimes cloying and often selfishly-emotional influence and demands that some family groups generate. The present generally low level of spiritual maturity exhibited by human societies today is clearly demonstrated by the fact that, for many people, only race and ethnicity are the main considerations in their relationships with others. This lack of understanding for the deeper and finer qualities ensures that this superficiality places outward appearances such as skin colour, race, physical looks, fashion and religion etc.. foremost.

Spiritual knowledge, particularly the right knowledge of The Law of Rebirth, will show the relative unimportance of such things as a person's race or nationality. The basis for assessing the worth of a human being can then be made on character alone. The following Biblical quotation probably best encapsulates this:

> "A useful tree cannot produce bad fruit; nor can a worthless tree produce good fruit. Every tree not producing good fruit will be felled and used as firewood. Reject their produce; for by this you can recognise them."
>
> (Matthew 7:18-20, Fenton.)

0.4.3 Families and Children.

The ramifications posed by the question of how and why particular souls incarnate into certain family groupings under "The Law of Attraction..." are so far reaching that if humanity were to *truly know* and **live** this knowledge, much of society's ugly side could be made non-existent – in perhaps just a few generations. Whilst that may seem a very broad statement, an examination of the serious importance of it and the equally grave responsibility attached to it should become evident to the open-minded reader, more especially if one is a parent, or wishes to become one. Since procreation is very much the norm rather than the exception, the significance of our opening sentence should be of primary interest to this group particularly.

Who has not heard the statement at some time, often given as an emotional outburst: "I didn't ask to be born!" – or: "I didn't choose my parents!" Unfortunately, **not so!** Notwithstanding that reality, it is nevertheless not an uncommon utterance, particularly from the young who may be subject to spiritually-wrong family constraints at the time that natural development calls them to enter the phase of adulthood and independence. Random selection does not operate here, but under the determination of one's free will, The Laws of "Attraction", "Reciprocal Action" and "Spiritual Gravity" most certainly do. These Laws basically determine the geographical location, the particular family of "lawful choice" and all other circumstances into which one is born. For an act of procreation simply provides *an opportunity* for *individual souls in the "beyond" to incarnate on earth.*

Since there are many souls awaiting such an opportunity, certain precise factors will finally bring the "correct one" to the prospective mother. The kind of soul that eventually incarnates, crucially governed by Spiritual Law, is determined by the family *environment* and connections to the *pregnant mother,* particularly. Strong similarities between the incoming soul and the mother or other members of the family may also have a bearing on *who* finally arrives. Or perhaps the prospective soul may have ties to a particular person or group of people that the prospective mother has close connections with. That potential can act as a powerful force of attraction for the souls surrounding her who are awaiting an opportunity to incarnate. Thus women, who are the providers of the "spiritual bridge" and are the **primary link** by which incoming souls are able to enter the earth plane, have a very great responsibility here.

Past life connections to various members of the family can be a strong determinant as well, and one which may later provide either harmonious relationships, or severely strained ones, depending on the circumstances of the past association. In all cases, however, the particular soul that finally inhabits the growing foetus will have been strictly determined according to Spiritual Law. And will thus possess all the necessary characteristics to be able to fulfil its particular role and purpose within the family grouping and in its own *personal* life-path as well.

The entry of the soul into the growing foetus, also determined by Law, takes place about the middle of pregnancy. [9] The seal of attraction is then complete and the soul takes full possession of its new home – the growing body in the mother's womb. She might well have mixed feelings, which may range from bliss to unease. This will depend on the nature of this *new stranger* she is *compelled to accept*.

The emotionally-charged issue of abortion takes on an entirely different hue when viewed from the perspective of Spiritual Law. According to the Eternal Laws by which we are granted life and sustenance, abortion is not the automatic right of any mother at any time during pregnancy. Of course, there will always occur certain life-threatening situations that may necessitate the need for difficult decisions in this respect. But the strident cry of: "My body, my right!", does not remove the Spiritual consequences wrought through unnecessary abortions by all involved – for there *is* "freedom of choice" here too. However, in both freedom of choice and the so-called *right* to "abortion on demand", those spiritual consequences nevertheless remain.

Even a purely foetal abortion – in the early stages of pregnancy before the entry of the soul – does not absolve the participants of the spiritual repercussions of such an act. From the waiting soul's point of view, all its hopes and aspirations for that particular earth life with its chosen parents, and the mutual opportunities of spiritual growth for both parties, is effectively lost. Whether or not a second opportunity for incarnation might present itself for the *same players* via another pregnancy could only be determined under the outworking of Spiritual Law.

Abortion after the entry of a soul into the growing foetus is similar to physical murder under those very exacting Laws of Creation, **regardless of what the medical profession, women's groups, or the lawmakers have determined for themselves**. It is a foolish delusion to believe that the act of ending the life of a human being as a purely "convenient solution" would not carry *serious spiritual consequences* for the perpetrators. Consequences,

---

[9]This entry time has been corroborated, **unknowingly**, by Dr. Robert Winston (of "The Human Body" fame). His statement to this effect was made in Part 1 of his *new series* of Human Development. That series traces the birth, life and development of a group of newborn babies to adulthood. His observations of major changes around the time of mid-pregnancy – which his narration outlined – indicated that much more happens in, and to, a growing foetus than just a continuation of normal physical development within the womb. Thus what Spiritual Law inviolably states, medical science has now noted – albeit unwittingly at this time.

moreover, that impact upon *all* who *support* such practices.[10]

The birth of handicapped children is therefore not without purpose either, whether for the mother, the family or, not least, for the handicapped one. Because these events are strictly governed by Spiritual Law, it is only through the knowledge of them that full understanding can be gained as to why such an event will visit itself upon a family group. It is surely certain, however, that in the caring of the handicapped one, the nature of the handicap will allow both family partners the necessary spiritual experiencing for which the birth was perhaps ordained. Permitted, moreover, through the *free-will decision of the parents for sexual union* thus leading to the ensuing procreative event. In this case, it is important to understand that it is only the physical body that is handicapped. The inner, animating core of the spirit, the real child and adult, is never so!

In similar vein, the infertility of certain couples is also not an arbitrary act. The inability to naturally produce offspring is similarly governed by "Spiritual Law". In other words, there will be a very good reason for this, even if not readily apparent. It may well have its origin in the long distant past, with its reciprocal effect translating in a deep desire to want children in the present, but not easily being able to, or possibly not at all, even with modern medical procedures. Infertile couples should thus determine whether or not it is within their ordained life-path to pursue parenthood. It could mean that having no children might allow them to fulfil a particular purpose more completely, whereas having children may make it much more difficult, or even impossible.

A more enlightened attitude would see couples planning for children solely from the *spiritual point of view*. Where no children are desired, conception would simply be avoided. The very nature of physical desire between couples, which should be viewed as both natural and special, means that the possibility of pregnancy is ever-present. With an understanding of the processes that determine the kind of new family addition that could arrive, however, future

---

[10]It is interesting to objectively observe the plight of certain peoples today whose *primary method* of birth control is abortion. The acceptance of this kind of birth-control regime, in the case of very populous countries, translates to hundreds of thousands, possibly millions, of destroyed lives over many years. The now more rapid reciprocal effect of all *spiritual* transgressions accelerates the consequences of this particular practice in such societies. The subsequent accelerating deterioration of the *material* and *social* environment of such nations is hardly surprising because the whole land becomes a vast, "reciprocal-reaping collective" for the particular peoples concerned.

prospective parents will be better able to plan for the reception of children who will be more aware and enlightened then might otherwise be the case without this new knowledge.

Just as the new soul will provide certain experiences and lessons for the family group into which it has incarnated, its new family and circumstances will offer similar provision for what it will need for its spiritual growth too. Viewed in this light, the wish to want a child should be more seriously considered because such a desire should be tempered by the acceptance of the responsibility to provide the correct upbringing for any offspring. Children are not ours to own and neither should we see them as arriving to us as a completely clean slate upon which we can write our own personal program for them.

With each act of procreation, the opportunity is offered for a soul to reside with us until such time as its ordained path or personal choices calls it to travel its own individual journey. If we have attracted spiritually and guided well, "offspring" should naturally develop the inner urge to make good decisions for themselves whenever crossroads are reached. Hopefully, the decision made then will be in accordance with the Eternal Laws, thus ensuring a good return for those we have nurtured and set free.

Under the outworking of this "attracting-process" a family of noble people will generally attract noble souls. The arrival of a so-called "black sheep" might indicate that the pregnant woman may have allowed a less than honourable person into her immediate sphere of influence *around the time of the entry of the soul.* **Under the Eternal Laws, a darker soul seeking to incarnate onto the earth plane will always drive back a lighter, more noble soul seeking the same opportunity.** This is purely the lawful effect of The Law of Spiritual Gravity.

Perhaps earlier generations intuitively understood this process in part, in determining pregnancy as a time, or term, "of confinement", thus as a period of "protective separation" from detrimental influences of society. This custom would offer natural spiritual protection, more especially up to the entry of the soul into the foetus. It is unlikely, however, that "modern feminist views" would accept such an assertion. Nevertheless, these strict and lawful "spiritual" processes cannot be circumvented by so-called "modern, enlightened attitudes" – social or medical![11]

---

[11] We may note this spiritually-cleansing preparation-time around the incarnation of Jesus. There, the Annunciation by the Messenger to Mary helped her to *prepare* her spirit and body for the reception of His Divine Core during

The effect of "The Law of Attraction..." around families and crime has produced some interesting statistics. Police records in many countries have recorded whole families – even generations of families – where crime in its myriad forms is regarded as the norm by such groups of wrong-thinking people. Sometimes, however, even in that kind of situation and against all the odds, a member of such a "family" may choose to follow a different path. Thus the more noble and spiritual characteristics of compassion, courage, inherent respect for justice and inner grace, for example, are *not* biologically inherited. Similarly, the uglier traits of humankind are not inherited either.

Nevertheless, it is still The Law of Attraction of Similar Species that primarily determines the make-up of families. Therefore, it should not be presumed that a soul with an innate propensity to live a less than noble existence on the earth must necessarily do so. Our inherent free-will factor gives such a person the opportunity to break free from any base propensities, no matter how strong, *if it so chooses or wills for itself*.

Genetic processes, which are by no means accidental, are what give rise to the physical characteristics of parental offspring. The Law of Reciprocal Action ensures that in such situations only those who have "sown the appropriate seeds" are incarnated into families and places where they are bound to enjoy genetic advantage or, conversely, suffer from hereditary handicap. By way of example, as a given disease is conquered in a particular part of the world, those souls whose karma *might* need the actual experience of that disease will only be able to incarnate in a country where it still exists.

In the light of this knowledge, we should re-examine our current thinking as to who or what actually constitutes a "victim". The present day tyranny of the "poor victim of circumstance" syndrome virtually allows some people of this mind-set to commit even crimes of shocking violence under the umbrella of this excuse. In truth, such terribly wrong attitudes debilitate and spiritually degrade society. We should recognise this for the wrong attitude, the "emotional disease", that it actually is and set up re-education programmes to smartly correct such incorrect, aspiritual thinking.

That is not to say, however, that help should not be offered to those in need. On the contrary, with this correct knowledge, *exactly the right kind of help* or education can be given, thus allow-

---

the pregnancy.

ing for the possibility of the complete elimination of this societal "illness". This would provide the necessary foundation for nobleness and *individual responsibility* to become the norm instead of the present practice of socially or culturally entrenching the totally wrong idea of "non-responsibility" into the very people who desperately need a complete change of thinking.

Consider, also, if the earth could be rid of all diseases and the causes of human suffering, any souls that needed to experience such suffering would not have the opportunity to be able to incarnate here. Consequently, we can further extrapolate that if we – all humanity – really strove to be truly noble in all our thoughts, words, aspirations and activities etc., it would become impossible for any unworthy spirits to incarnate on earth simply because *the connecting bridge of attraction* would not be there. Through this recognition and process, a more enlightened humankind could make the earth what it was originally ordained to be – *a paradise*. More to the point, that is what could and should have happened. Our choice and our responsibility solely, however.

To this end it is important to understand that the present thrust of globally entrenching the concept of "my rights", transgresses virtually every aspect of Spiritual Law. Almost nowhere now do we hear of responsibilities, duties, or obligations. We hear only the increasingly strident and selfish cry of **"my rights"**! In the case of the relationship between parents and children, this translates into a mad tyranny where children's *rights* have become more important than their *responsibilities*. Just as parents have responsibilities to their offspring so, too, should children be taught to fulfil this aspect of Spiritual Law.

By first putting in place the attitude of responsibilities and duties to each other, we automatically create an environment where rights can become synonymous with duties, for under Spiritual Law fulfilment of duty and responsibility must come before any claim to rights. Therefore, children can only claim rights if they loyally perform their duties.

0.4.4 Why there is so much Violence and Evil on Earth. The "Divine Warning" to Mothers!

The ultimate reason for the huge levels of violence committed by evil men upon their fellow men today is not necessarily because of religious, political or geo-political considerations; or ethnic or racial tension; or wealth versus poverty or any other *excuse*. Those are simply the societal or religious parameters that offer the framework under which such people can carry out their evil works. The *true* answer lies in the knowledge and outworking of The Spiritual Laws/Principles. The problem today – which has nevertheless been with us for a long time now – is precisely about; —

— *the kinds of human souls permitted entry onto the Earth from darker regions in the beyond to whom fellow humans on Earth should <u>never</u> have stretched a hand.*

Quite simply, through the justly lawful process of procreation and incarnation under the aegis and outworking of "The Law of Attraction...", particularly, **doors have long been opened to the lower regions of the beyond.** The huge numbers of the more evil-minded human souls forced to be there under the *immutable outworking* of "The Law of Spiritual Gravity" (explained further on in this segment) are offered a *bridge* by which they can return to Earth. These bridges of attraction, in the very first instance, **are the mothers of the various global communities into which such souls incarnate.**

We speak of responsibility as being one of the key factors for creating a better society, *but ignorantly refuse to accept, or even believe in, the very kind of ultimate responsibility that would prevent such dark humans from arriving on Earth to wreak murderous havoc in their later years.*

The main contributing factors here are the **terrible distortions** of the original religious teachings given to mankind over millennia. Such twisting of the clear original sets the parameters whereby **whole societies today now live their respective delusions about the absolute rightness of their particular religion, solely.** Within those societies the children, *especially*, are naturally significantly-exposed from birth to every nuance of societal or cultural interpretation of the particular **religion** into which they are born.

If we examine revelatory prophecy very objectively, we may note [from Chapter 1 of the Parent Work] in —

Crucial Imperative No. 8:

> That we, the human Beings of planet Earth, *inherently possess* the ordained *attribute* of *"free-will"*. That *not understanding* the so-called inequities or injustices of life has its *genesis* in human *non-recognition* and thus *non-understanding* of this most **"Crucial Imperative"**.

— we discover a very compelling reason [***freedom of choice***] why a comprehensive and terrible *"cleansing"* is virtually the only solution left to prevent wrong religious and cultural teachings from permitting the entry of evil-minded souls onto the Earth in the future. Such a final end will bring to a juddering halt any further opportunity for the evil-minded to incarnate here. For, quite obviously, *many* of the women of the world – from birth inculcated with the particular "mind-set" of the various races, cultures and religions ***into which they had <u>chosen</u> to incarnate*** and who therefore ***primarily*** provide *the bridge of attraction* to waiting souls – ***will not be here either.***

The reader should seriously **dwell awhile here** and strive to understand <u>why</u> **Jesus, The Son of God**, should so strongly warn His Disciples in the *way* that He did, when *they* asked Him to tell *them* what would come upon the Earth and humankind at the closing of the age – these times now!
A specific, <u>Divine</u>, and very blunt warning goes out to the <u>women</u> who will be <u>mothers</u> at the time. From Matthew 24:19-22, Fenton:

> "But **alas for those <u>with child</u> and those <u>who nurse</u> in those days**! Pray, however, that your flight may not come during the winter, nor upon a Rest-day; for there shall ***then*** be **wide-spread affliction, such as has not been known since the beginning of the world until now**, no, nor will ***ever*** be known again. And if those times were not cut short, *not a man would be saved*; but for the sake of the chosen ones, those times will be cut short.

The Book of Mark states the warning equally strongly.

> "But **alas for those <u>with child</u>, and for the <u>nursing women</u> in those days**! And pray especially that your

flight may not take place during the winter. For in those days there will be affliction, such as has **never been known since the beginning of the creation which God created until now, and such as shall never be again**. And unless the Lord had cut short those times, *none could be saved*;...

(Mark 13:17-20, Fenton.
All emphases mine.)

Even on His grievous, agonising walk to His execution at Golgotha, more warnings to women:

> And a large crowd of the people followed Him, including women, who were beating their breasts, and lamenting Him. Jesus, however, turning towards them, said, "Daughters of Jerusalem, weep not for me; but weep for yourselves and for your children. For now the days are coming, during which they shall say, Happy are the barren, happy the childless, and happy those who have never nursed."

(Luke 23:26-31, Fenton.)

The *clear warning* to the women at "the end of the times" also strongly hints that the destructive period will come upon the world suddenly and unexpectedly, but last only for a relatively short time. Hence his further warning that the period of destruction would therefore need to be on a scale "...not seen before, nor will be seen again", in order to *complete the job*. Thus the need to cut the times short or *no one* would be left.

Whilst the measure for interpreting Bible Scripture – particularly the words of Jesus as recorded in the Gospels – is often a very broad one with many offering their personal ideas on meaning, no interpretation of the *primary sentence directed towards women in the above quote* has thus far crossed the path of this writer. Since we have stated what will surely produce outcries of horror from women's groups and civil and human rights advocates as well, let us now analyse what that specific warning to the world's women – from the knowledge of the Highest of Law – *actually relates to*.

And given by One in Whom inherently resided exactly that Living Law.

[The whole thrust of this writing is to *enlighten* and *point the way* to that very **All-Truth** from which we derive the spiritual knowledge of **Creation-Law** so written herein!]

Therefore, in terms of a soul incarnating to a mother *anywhere* in the world, to *any* culture, race or religion; the **primary aspect** of the event is that the **new-born** is **not** the **personal property** of the mother, the associated family, or the particular group into which it is born. In the very first instance, it is its *own individual person.* It is a *singularly individual spirit* which has journeyed through this part of Creation *primarily for its spiritual purpose.* The various families *into which* it had previously and successively *incarnated* under the absolute immutability of the key Laws of "Attraction..." and "Rebirth", **unequivocally reveal** that it is **not** the property of anyone else.

New-born babies are very much welcomed, nurtured and protected by most mothers of the world, and strong bonding is a natural and desirable feature of the mother/baby relationship. That we certainly agree is absolutely the right thing. However, since we are assessing **the actual meaning of Christ's warning to mothers at this end-time**, then other, more powerful considerations must come into play here if there is to be any kind of logical meaning according to the outworking of "The Spiritual Laws of Life":
— **CREATION-LAW!**.

The deaths of babies and children invariably strike a painful chord in most people. That is because the vast majority of adult human beings only see the *physical* happening; the death of a small, vulnerable and often helpless little person. What we do not see is that which is *released* from that small body; the *actual person* – the *spirit* who would have grown to adulthood – now *free* of the body, but at a tender age, however. Sometimes the loss is so great for the nurturing mother who carried and delivered the soul into the world that her emotional grief may be inconsolable. Therein, however, **rests the substantive meaning of the warning to women.**

Thus, the gift of a child is exactly that – a gift. Inviolable Spiritual Law unequivocally states that children may arrive *when least expected or planned for* and, as is painfully obvious to all, **can be taken at any time without the parent's permission being sought.**

So the loss of any child should be *spiritually understood* to have been a gift for whatever time *was ordained for it*; particularly for the mother, but also for the wider family. Oftentimes at the moment of greatest grief – unfortunately too often – blame is sought for the loss. Regrettably, therefore, if that blame should be directed towards The One Who gave Life to all anyway, *including* the grieving mother, then the outworking of The Law of Reciprocal Action must, and *will*, run its eventual course.

In the case of catastrophe-related destruction of global societies and their human populations – and also because the demographics of the Earth's population show a large proportion now quite young – any destructive effects may impact on this group perhaps disproportionately. One can readily understand the prophecy where, at that time, "great wailing and gnashing of teeth" will occur. The Indian Ocean tsunami tragedy is a case in point; so much outpouring of aid globally, but so many children dead and so much inconsolable grief and anguish. The same was experienced by Chinese mothers as a result of China's 2008 earthquake. There, however, a harder dimension because of that country's "one-child" policy.

The one element in what we are stating that *could* serve to *help* mothers, particularly, over the loss of children is the lawful fact that babies and young children, because they have **not** reached the age of spiritual responsibility, are **not so subject** to the outworking of The Law of Reciprocal Action – the **'Iron Law' of Karma**. Therefore, unlike adults who *are* so subject to that *full* outworking – and who thus are lawfully propelled to that Plane which *they* had prepared *for themselves* – babies and children, precisely in accordance with the Perfect Justice of The Spiritual Laws, will find themselves in one of the 'Lighter Planes'. There to be cared for and undergo growth and development alongside *other* human spirits *also residing there*.

The clear connotation here, in concert with the warning of Jesus to mothers, is **to seek out and strive to understand the knowledge of The Eternal Laws.** So that, should the situation arise where a mother must *let go* one she has brought into the world, she will do so *with **understanding gratitude*** to He Who granted her the ability to **bear** *the child in the first place*, and gratitude ***for the time*** *she was permitted to be with that soul.* As previously stated, for those who would curse in hate or anger, The Law must, and will, bring the reciprocal effect! Such inviolable, Lawful, outworking simply cannot be altered!

That is precisely why it is stated that the millennial phase will be one of peace ***for the few who are left***. In the first instance, it will be forced upon those who survive through the discipline of *adjusting* to The Laws as they actually are; as we should have done long ago. Secondly, those *who would have* refused to bend or bow will simply *not be here*. Given the increasing levels of evil and bloodshed that men are visiting upon each other now, it is unlikely that such dark practices will be permitted to continue for very much longer. Only when the evil-minded, *through their **personal** choices*, have self-destructed, will there then be peace and harmony for the few left on Earth.

That is why it is also stated that the Earth will be cleansed so comprehensively; and cleansed through the outworking of Perfect and Just Laws! After that period, human offspring will be born healthier and more spiritually-aware, because there will not be any dark souls incarnating onto the Earth again. For human mothers, the births of the new-born will no longer carry with it the pain of childbirth as has long been the case. In concert with the subject matter here, this key question arises.

Why have human mothers suffered so much during a process that should really be a defining moment of blissful joy — without pain?

0.4.5 The Universal Pain of Childbirth. The Enlarging Baby Cranium: A Medical "Mystery".

Whilst touching on the phenomenon of ***the enlarging baby cranium***, this sub-Section mainly assesses the aspects of, and reasons for, the ***universal pain of childbirth*** for birthing mothers. So whilst primarily concerned with the *pain* of childbirth, we also necessarily connect to a corresponding and following *linking* segment: **The Enlarging Baby Cranium: The "Lawful" Reason.**

In the final analysis, even though these two aspects are intrinsically connected by virtue of the origin of firstly the universal pain of childbirth and secondly the enlarging baby cranium, it does not at all mean that birthing pain is *caused* by the phenomenon of enlarging craniums – though of course it can be. The seeming paradox here is that ***despite*** their inherently-close association with regard to the ***genesis*** of ***both*** aspects, they ***could*** nonetheless be ***construed*** as stemming from ***different*** beginnings – i.e., in terms of what we will reveal as the ***actual*** reason/s for ***both***.

With the pain of childbirth now universally accepted as being very normal, women individually, women's groups, and all of the medical profession dealing in obstetrics especially, should *really* consider *why* that is so. Or perhaps even why that *need* be so.

As a writer who occupies the male end of the gender spectrum, I am sure that many women will be amazed at the sheer effrontery of my comments. For what would a mere man know of a woman's feelings and emotions in childbirth? Of course that is absolutely correct *insofar* as the physical and emotional experience is concerned, and I am sure that no man would ever *presume* to know. However, what we can never push away is the clear fact that the 'mechanics' of the process which occurs from conception to birth takes place under the aegis of precise, non-negotiable, *non-emotional,* **Creation-Law parameters**. So irrespective of what we may wish to place on childbirth, women's notions and feelings, father's notions and feelings, philosophical, cultural or social beliefs and commentary, etc., the fact will forever remain that the path from conception to birth – even if generated by in-vitro fertilisation – is, *unarguably*, absolutely subject to **Immutable Creation-Law.**

On the question of 'birthing pain', therefore: It is well known that the contractions necessary to propel the baby toward birth are painful for all women, never mind an enlarging baby cranium to complicate matters further for some. And even though the *pain-threshold* for birthing mothers would obviously vary, the 'normal' human birthing process associated with 'labour' and 'delivery' nonetheless produces pain for all, so epidurals are common. Therefore, especially centred on that reality, what we state explanatorily in the ***two linking sub-Sections*** to *be* the *actual reason/s* for the high pain levels *and* enlarging baby cranium will most certainly be branded ridiculous, trite, foolish, uninformed and/or uneducated to the point of being ignorant, totally unscientific — and perhaps even dangerously religious. And thus will surely offend many!

The opposite, however, stands as The Truth here!

>For no matter how many times in the Parent Work and in this Booklet we *necessarily repeat* the following clear and unarguable fact, it will not *yet* find easy accommodation with the educational establishment, *particularly.* So therefore once more:
>
>The present, deplorable state of global societies *unequivocally testifies* to the *sure reality* that we human beings not only ***do not*** live according to the true and

absolutely inviolable **Creation Laws of Life**, but each generation born travels further and further ***from them***. The responsibility for that resultant non-recognition can be laid squarely at the feet of *aspiritual* education parameters leading to a crucially-dangerous lack of *genuine life-knowledge*. That reality has been instrumental in the commission of increasingly darker deeds by the many millions born year by year. Now, finally, we are brought face to face with our foolish arrogance. The previous sub-section explained the **HOW**.

Now we will explain the **WHY**. Firstly, however, let us *seriously* stress the fact that the actual answer to both our present questions — and I can hear many disbelieving cries of; "Oh no, not more religious rubbish." — really is in that especial **"Primary Book of Foundational-Science": The Bible!**

In the Parent Work we explain, in a very basic way, the nonetheless step-by-stupendous-step of the complete Creation-process beginning with the *immediate creation* of male and female in **The First Creation**. Then very much later in **Subsequent Creation**, the "coming into being", the *forming*, of animal-man "from out of the dust of the ground". Finally, the *entry* of the human-spiritual aspect *into* those prepared primate vessels which *thereby* permitted and facilitated *our human* growth and development to this present, 21st-century evolutionary point.

Human reproductive ability subsequently burdened an Earth groaning at the seams with a population now set to surpass the 7 billion mark. With it, however, a cranial *abberation* in foetal development. The clues to the resolution of both the problems we address in this sub-Section may be found in specific texts in **The Book of Genesis** under the sub-heading:

The Temptation Of Eve.

The story of Adam and Eve, whilst taken *literally* by many millions, should really be understood as being *more symbolic* of the *entry* of sin into the world. In other words; *a free-will choice producing a specific outcome under the inviolable outworking of* **The Law of Reciprocal Action.**

In the context of the two questions we address here – the universally tolerated 'birthing pains' and the enlarging baby cranium which medical science is currently puzzling over – certain key Scriptures unequivocally answer the question of pain. They also, paradoxically, offer *the clues* that *link* to the following segment; which *there* provides the *complete reason* for the growing problem of the enlarging cranium in human babies.

So: The **singular reason** for Eve being commanded *not to eat* [ingest] of *just one* particular tree in the Garden of Eden lies in the *effect* that *that particular fruit* had upon her and Adam once they had *tasted* [ingested] it.
From Genesis 3:1-7, Fenton: The tempting serpent asks Eve:[12]

> "Is it true that GOD has said, you may not eat of every tree of the Garden?"
> And the woman replied to the serpent, "We may eat of the fruit of the trees of the garden; but of the fruit of the tree which is in the middle of the garden, GOD has said, 'do not eat of it, and do not even touch it, *lest you die'*."
> But the serpent answered the woman: "You will not die; but GOD knows that at the time you eat of it, your eyes will then be opened, and you will be like GOD, acquainted with both good *and evil*."
> So the woman *perceiving* that the tree was *good for food*, [tasty] and *beautiful to the eyes* [alluring], and a tree **stimulating** to the **intellect**, she took some of its fruit and ate it, and gave some to her husband with her; and he also ate it.
> Then the eyes of both of them *were opened*...
>
> Emphases and parenthetic additions mine.

The key point here centres on the well-known fact that for we humans, forbidden fruit is invariably perceived as *tasty*, *alluring*, and *stimulating* to certain senses in an *inappropriate* way, or *stimulating* for the *wrong reason/s*. Therefore, the notion that an *actual reptile* tempted Eve does not at all hold up to just plain and simple logic. And **Creation-Law** cannot be anything other than logical; either in its "Form" and "Essence", or in its *inviolable outworking*. The 'serpent' that enticingly tempts humankind is the quiet, insidious, ever-so-seductive voice which the *'inner' spiritual conscience* strives to warn against, but which the *'outer' worldly intellectual human entity* invariably ignores.

---

[12]Eve: *Khavah*, or *life-container*.

So to taste of *fruit* that will bring **spiritual** death is simply to choose a path that *opposes* **The Spiritual Laws of Creation**; thus one that *no longer* adheres to a *spiritual* way, but is the chosen [by humankind] *intellectual* way. [The way of the 'shrewdly-calculating' intellect.]

To repeat: Eve [humankind] rejected the [correct] *spiritual way* and chose, instead, the alluring *intellectual way* – **solely**. Now it is "the way of the world" with all its attendant aspiritual garbage and increasing problems. We therefore *sowed the wind* in the [female] *decision*, but now *reap the whirlwind* – primarily for women in this case – in the [female] *outcome*. For in Genesis 3:16, Fenton (emphases mine), we read:

> But to the woman He said, "I will increase your sorrows and your joys. *You will give birth to children* <u>**with pain**</u>;..."

Of all creatures on Earth human woman, certainly, is burdened with painful birth of offspring. Whilst other life-forms *can* have difficult births, for the most part they go about their birthing-business with relative ease and few complications. Rather than being a *relatively* uncomplicated, *natural* event, human birthing has virtually become a 'medical' procedure with, at times, a whole team of medical staff actively involved. Of course that is exactly right if there are complications, but the development and necessity for there to be specialist wards in modern hospitals as the accepted norm now seems to be a 'reversal' of what should be more a 'natural order'.

In the case of serious birthing difficulties, both the affected mother and attending obstetrics professionals really need to take into account the knowledge and outworking of **The Spiritual Laws of Creation**. For within certain specific and connecting Laws therein will often be found the *actual* reason for such traumatic births. In other words, irrespective of what the physical or medical considerations might indicate for the particular problem or for the mother, certain connecting links between her and the newly emerging soul may hold the deeper reason. In such cases, the *medical* situation will simply *parallel* the final *outworking* of the more decisive *spiritual* aspect.

The question of the enlarging baby cranium is one that Western obstetrics' specialists and researchers, particularly, are currently striving to answer. The equation is quite simple, though of course problematic: An *enlarging* baby cranium needing to exit the womb through a pelvic girdle that is *not* enlarging. The natural accompaniment is the potential for increased pain and a longer time in labour. Now why should that be? What factor or factors prevent such a logical accommodation? Why will Mother Nature not provide the obvious solution; hold the cranium to a size that is exactly right for natural, uncomplicated and *relatively* painless childbirth for human mothers?

For that is the case with millions of herd animals that must give birth quickly and easily for simple survival of their offspring which must be ready to run with the herd just hours after birth. Natural predators 'sort out' any problematic births. Certainly in the wild with mammals that produce multiple births [a 'litter' of wolf pups for example], the females usually give birth easily, lick the litter clean and suckle them immediately. And without any requirement for 'extra care'.

Where human interference in the form of specific breeding occurs, however, there we may see birthing problems, but not of the animals making. A case in point is the English bulldog. Bred for bull-baiting, the now too-large-head is so problematic for the birthing bitch that 95% of births are cesarean. Free whelping is not recommended.

> **Note:** Given the very contentious nature of this subject, the **female** reader, **most especially**, must understand that we are *not comparing* the birthing experience of human mothers with that of other mammals. What we are explaining here is an *outcome* for our *human* species that animals — by virtue of the fact that they inherently possess the attribute of *instinct* only and **not** *free will* — could *never ever* set in train. So it is crucially important to withhold judgement here until one has *read through* the full, *explanatory*, texts.

At first glance, therefore, a connection between a recently recognised medical problem [perhaps more relevant with Western birth-mothers] and **Human Language** may seem tenuous at best and perhaps even rather silly at worst. However, as we state throughout the far more comprehensive Parent Work, it is *not possible* for there *not* to be answers to the questions that affect we humans *on Earth*. In this particular case, the *actual* reason/s will certainly *not fit* with accepted medical-science protocols [or even beliefs] in *either* research *or* "best practice parameters" in modern-day, first-world obstetrics.

Nonetheless, there *is* an answer. Moreover, not only *is* there an answer to both the subjects under consideration here, it *is* **in** **The Bible**! And it is an answer/reason in exact concert with the great and inviolable **Law of Reciprocal Action** — *The Iron Law of Sowing and Reaping*. [We of the human species will yet learn that we simply *cannot* transgress **Creation-Law** with impunity and still believe there are no *consequences* from doing so. The *greater* the degree of transgressing, the *more severe* the consequential outcome – as has *resulted* from these two problems.]

Now, precisely *because* the enlarging baby cranium aspect centres on the skeletal frame of the human being, the *actual answer* in the final analysis *automatically* incorporates ***scientific*** realities.

So why should a completely natural process become so problematic for humans that more and more 'C sections' are performed for all sorts of reasons? An increasing number are, of course, elective; but that is not the main consideration.

Here is the primary issue once again: In more or less 'evolutionary' terms, why has the brain case of the human baby enlarged to such a degree that the head size in relation to body size is now so disproportionately big at birth that it can pose serious problems for delivery?

The *actual* and thus *ultimate cause* of this 'medical' quandary in humans centres precisely on our wonderful *gift* and *inherent* attribute of *free-will*. Therein lies the paradox. Animals etc., by virtue of having no such attribute, cannot possibly ever be similarly burdened. We of global humanity, however, having *long-chosen* our path, are now *reaping* the consequential outcomes in the present.

There is the *primary* answer for the *spiritually-perceptive* reader; but probably not for the *non* spiritually-*receptive* intellectual. The intellect of man, whilst absolutely necessary for tasks on Earth, has no *perceptive* spiritual capacity *whatsoever*, so has no affinity with higher *Spiritual knowledge*. That is why many noted and lauded 'intellectuals', in commentary and/or in their writings, rail against the reality or even *notion* of 'inviolable absolutes' such as **Creation-Law** and **Spiritual Truth**.

The terrible but nonetheless *self-wrought* tragedy *resulting* from this non-recognition and non-acceptance – and thus rejection of *immutable* **Creation-Law Truth** by the very people who, educationally, sway hundreds of millions to *their* non-recognition – is a world blind to the very knowledge that could 'turn things around'.

Isaiah, the great 'Old Testament Prophet', long ago warned that humankind would reach this very point we are now *fruitlessly* struggling with. **WHY?**
Specifically for scientists, educationalists, theologians, noted intellectuals – and also *for birthing mothers today* – **Isaiah again speaks:**

> "The 'Earth' also is ***defiled*** under the ***inhabitants*** thereof; because ***they*** have
> ***transgressed*** the Laws,
> ***changed*** the decrees,
> ***broken*** the everlasting covenant.
> Therefore has the ***curse*** devoured the 'Earth', and those that dwell therein ***are desolate***:..."
>
> (Isaiah 24:5-6, Fenton. Emphases mine.)

[We previously stated that the whole picture of the enlarging baby cranium has precise resonance with, and to, human language. So the concomitant and *complete* reason for this abberation is reproduced here from the Parent Work: **Bible "Mysteries" Explained.** Specifically Chapter 8 **The Emergence of Language.** Sub-Chapter: **The Biblical "Fall of Man"; A Disastrous Legacy for Global Humanity**; sub-Section, **The Enlarging Baby Cranium: The "Reason".**]

0.4.6 The Enlarging Baby Cranium: The "Lawful" Reason!

> This sub-Section connects to the previous *linking* segment. Here we provide the *full linking knowledge* to *especially explain* the **why** of the enlarging baby cranium.

In concert with the discussion of the moment, the question of what exactly constitutes our human ***life-force*** needs to be brought into this analysis. As we have noted in a number of places in the Parent Work, that dynamic is either an animating power *separate from* the human body – which is *our* absolute conviction – or it is a *non-separable*, ***solely material***, 'life-force' inherently-fused into every cell nucleus throughout the whole human system. Thus for empirical science, a genomic lattice-work completely permeating every part of the entire body that, in a computer-like way, controls, regulates and maintains all bodily processes. Yet, in what would then be the most *illogical* association of all *if* such *really* were the case, to *also* possess the ability to somehow still make ***free-will*** decisions.

As stated in "**Author's Note**" and in Chapter 2; "**The Origins of Man: Genesis and Science Agree**" of the Parent Work, National Geographic Channel queried *exactly* this 'life-force' question in two separate Documentaries: "**Birth of Life**", and "**Human Ape**". The associated and most relevant point asked was:
"How did *non-living* material come to life?"

The History Channel, too, seeks the same kind of definitive answer. The series, "**How Life Began**", asks:
"Where did [this] life come from? What IS life, exactly?"

And in a *space* of perhaps *insightful prescience*, the Series further and *crucially* queries:
"*Is it chemical, spiritual, or a combination of both?*"

(All emphases mine.)

In 2009 Documentary Channels examined the phenomenon of the human baby's enlarging cranium. According to the various researchers interviewed, the baby's head will only fit through the pelvic girdle *one way*. So unless the baby receives a 'signal' to rotate its head to the right position as it approaches that point, the head – and therefore the rest of the body – will not get through the 'birth opening' of the pelvic girdle to transit into the birth canal. In some cases, evidently increasing, even that is no longer *naturally* possible for *some* mothers; thus requiring Cesarean deliveries for *every* baby born to them.

The question for medical researchers presently studying this 'development' must surely be: **Why**? Ordinarily, evolutionary-type processes – such as appears to be the case here – will ensure that development or change in one area will be matched by the appropriate 'developmental-response' in the correspondingly-affected area; for this is not a 'mutation'. In the case of the human female pelvic-girdle configuration, *continuing enlargement* of the birth baby's 'head space' to keep pace with an enlarging baby cranium would only be viable if we reverted back to the stronger skeletal structure of Neanderthals. However, the heavier bone required for larger pelvic girdles, thus leading to correspondingly larger hips, means much slower bi-pedal locomotion. An enlarging pelvic girdle in the finer skeleton of the modern female form would probably eventually result in a weakened skeletal structure, so would not be a good outcome in terms of optimal 'evolutionary' or 'growth' development to accommodate enlarging baby craniums.

The 'head rotation manoeuvre' that babies perform in order to exit the womb has produced two divergent opinions among researchers. One view holds that *that* has *always* been the case, whilst the opposite notion tends towards it being a more or less 'evolutionary' development now necessary for the mother to deliver the baby safely – precisely *because* the brain case has been gradually enlarging over a very long time. So even allowing for the relatively soft bones in the skull of babies which offers some degree of 'flexing' at birth; increasingly, according to some opinions, that is evidently still not sufficient to permit birth without the necessary 'head rotation'. Essentially, then, we have a situation where one part of this equation – the pelvic girdle of birth mothers – cannot *safely* keep developmental pace with the enlarging heads of babies.

As we have stated in the corresponding, *linking*, segment; Sub:
— **The Universal Pain of Childbirth. The Enlarging Baby Cranium: A Medical "Mystery"** and restate once more in reinforcement:

— "Why will Mother Nature not provide the obvious solution; hold the cranium to a size that is exactly right for natural, uncomplicated and *relatively* [though perhaps not completely] painless childbirth for human mothers?" Millions of herd animals must give birth quickly and easily for simple survival of the offspring which, in most cases, must be ready to run with the herd just hours after birth.

Why is this completely natural process becoming so problematic for humans that more and more 'C sections' are performed for all sorts of reasons? In *evolutionary* terms, why has the cranium of the human baby enlarged to such a degree that the head size in relation to body size is now so *disproportionately* big at birth that it can pose serious problems for delivery?

Echoing Einstein's deep understanding of where *real* knowledge *truly* comes from, the answer to the question we address in this segment can be *intuitively understood* from the explanations herein. We should note that the great man stated that he never came upon any of his discoveries;

'...through *rational* thinking'.

"And if one asks whence derives the authority of such fundamental ends, since they cannot be stated and justified merely by reason, one can only answer: they come into being *not through demonstration **but through revelation**, through the medium of powerful personalities.* One must not attempt to justify them, but rather to sense their nature simply and clearly."

"But science can only be created by those who are thoroughly imbued with the aspiration toward truth and understanding."

(Ideas and Opinions, p 42-3.
All emphases mine.)

The *reason* for the enlarging cranium in babies lies in the *seriously-aberrant **development***, over millennia, of the human brain. The *present-day* configuration of the two primary parts – the cerebrum and the cerebellum – hold the key to **why** the brain case is enlarged beyond its original, *lawfully-ordained*, structure.
The cerebrum: The large rounded structure of the brain occupying most of the cranial cavity, divided into two cerebral hemispheres. Commonly called the '*large brain*'. [Therein lies a clue.]
The cerebellum: [diminutive of cerebrum] Often referred to as the '*small brain*'. [There lies one other part to this "mystery".]
According to neurological research, the structure of the brain responsible for regulation and coordination of complex voluntary movement, lying below the occipital lobes of the cerebral hemispheres.

Empirical brain research, even though identifying and correlating individual areas of the brain to precise processes and functions within the human body, does not provide the *actual* answer to the enlarging cranium. Scientific literature notes that birthing by human mothers has always been more difficult than for other mammals due to narrow bi-pedal hips. These two seemingly-unrelated aspects nonetheless provide the connecting link to the question of the enlarging baby cranium. From all that we have explained thus far, the reason *should* be clear enough.
Question! **The brain**: Insufficient use — or over-use? Centred on that very question, let us itemise a few points that will help to both focus and clarify the direction we must take to understand and resolve this problem for science.

- "Use it or lose it"; a well known but nonetheless apt truism.
- Under-development stunts growth and creates imbalance.

- Over-development will also create imbalance, but of a different kind.

- Both those aspects of brain *activity* are thus an *abberation* by virtue of the resulting *imbalance aspect*.

So, over-development of *anything* in *any* field can result in unexpected outcomes and/or ones not necessarily commensurate with the original projected/assumed parameters for the particular thing. [In this modern era obsessed with the 'body beautiful', body-builders can develop any part of the body relatively easily. It is therefore possible to 'bulk-up', for example, just one arm to produce an *aberrant* form emulating the large protective claw that certain crabs possess – which is *natural* for *them*.]

As an historical engineering example, original designs for bulk carriers [ships] and a particular type of bridge worked perfectly well and safely when kept within *original*, specification parameters. However, when **modified beyond that safe original**, some failed; with resultant loss of life. We may ask: *'What has engineering got to do with brain-development?'* Well, the *principle* is no different. Develop **anything** beyond its original, **ordained purpose**, and it must obviously **fail** that purpose.

So is it with the human brain! The *over-development* of the *intellect* has resulted in the present-day, *aberrant* phenomenon of a brain-case enlarging to accommodate that greater and greater – and unfortunately much lauded and desired – intellectual capacity of *modern*, though now *very aspiritual*, man. Language, or more precisely the misuse of it, has been a *major driver* in this process. Man had two choices: Maintain the *spiritual power* that he *originally* imbued language with; or fall away from that vital life-connection and *subvert* and coarsen it with the *increasingly-dominant* aspiritual, *earthly* – and thus **Earth-bound** – intellect.

An important and related question is: 'How has this *distortion* from the time of the *story* of Eve's transgression carried itself down through the generations to the present?'
The step to that progression begins thus:

> But to the woman He said, "I will increase your sorrows and your joys. *You will give birth to children **with pain**;...*"
>
> (Genesis 3:16, Fenton. Emphases mine.)

The connecting answer to our associated query – which the non-Christian community will no doubt regard as religious claptrap – nonetheless *also* lies in The Bible. Notwithstanding the sure 'slings and arrows' of official academia, the *actual* reason for the present aberration yet resonates with very simple *scientific* principles. Once again, *over-development* is the key to understanding the secondary aspect of the overall 'enlarging-cranium' question. Now we get to the nub of the problem with regard to the primary subject matter of *this* segment.

The Bible speaks of, and strongly condemns, *the* 'Hereditary Sin' of mankind. The obvious pointer to **what** and **why** lies in the word 'hereditary', i.e., something 'passed on' – from one generation to the next. Equally obviously, that clearly cannot mean – again as so many otherwise well-intentioned Christians firmly believe – that we have *all inherited*, and are thus *all tainted*, by the so-called *original sin* of Adam and Eve. That *fundamentalist* tenet is so *completely* wrong, so plain silly, that any argument to support it simply *cannot* be made. For if it *were* correct, it would logically mean that we do *not* possess the attribute of 'free-will', and are thus subject to consequences *not* of our own making.

That is as illogical as it is ridiculous. Such a *distorted* concept of Truth does not even *begin* to resonate with the **Perfection** of **Creation-Law**. For we are warned that we must "reap what we sow" [but solely, *individually*, through *personal* choice/s], which even Christian fundamentalists cannot logically argue against.

For **Decisions** must *always* produce **Consequences!**

As with so many strongly-defended, so called, sacrosanct tenets and beliefs of global Christendom, the *terrible distortion* here lies in the *non-understanding* of *exactly* what was originally set in train by Eve's[13] [*humankind's*] serious act of disobedience: Thus what was passed on through the *generations* to the present-day to be now puzzled over by brain and obstetrics researchers.

Therefore, the *actual* transgression, as we once more explain, was *choosing* to *no longer follow* the original *spiritual* path *ordained* for earthly humanity *for all time*. The **sin** is represented by the *tasting* of the *forbidden* fruit, i.e., the 'falling away' *from* the ordained spiritual path with the *inevitable* and thus subsequent *over-strengthening* of the *worldly* intellect. The *serpent* in the story

---

[13]Eve: *Khavah*, or *life-container*.

represents the *insidious cunning* of the *Earth-bound*, therefore *aspiritual*, **intellect**!

What became – and actually *still is* – the *'hereditary aspect'*, is hereditary *solely because* the over-stimulation, the over-strengthening, of the intellect resulted in an *imbalance* of the once *equal-sized*, harmoniously-active *front and back brains*. Through millennia of *over-cultivation*, the consequently-developed far greater mass, the 'large brain' [***the intellectual brain***] now *almost completely fills* the brain case. The other *once complementary **spiritual** part*, now referred to as the '*small brain*', is completely **stunted** through **non-use**. With each generation born, therefore, the *intellectual* part of the brain grew *disproportionately larger*.

Stimulated through more and more *aspiritual* ways and ideas, particularly in education, that continual development meant that the *size* and *power* of the *intellectual part* of the brain *had to increase*. The resultant and inevitable legacy is, quite logically, the enlarged brain case evident today! Perhaps, to coin a 'today' phrase: "**Enlarged to the max.**"

We global participants of the aspiritual educational paradigm that has held sway for millennia – but now at its *greatest* strength – have *passed on* that aberration, **hereditarily**, to *all* successive generations in our individual genealogical lines. That very long process of *intellectual* over-stimulation resulted in the need for *more* room in the cranium. Even though enlarging only minutely-incrementally over millennia, the resultant outcome is sufficient to force the question **why** from the scientific community. Thus all of humankind is now affected by wrong ideas and teachings, and our earthly home contaminated by that **aspiritual poison**.

So, until and unless there is an immediate and very massive fundamental shift in the educational ethos that the ruling university elite clings to, the most that can be expected from that quarter is *more questions* producing *more research* to try to answer the next lot of **questions**. Never the final answer! But it keeps those presently in control forever in control, doesn't it?

Just as we have offered logical explanations for a number of scientific/religious questions as yet without definitive answers from those two Disciplines, so, too, has the quandary of the enlarging baby cranium also found logical resolution here.

Necessarily strongly-repeated in the Parent Work, only with the recognition and acceptance of the knowledge-aegis inherent in: —

Crucial Imperative No 2:

That we, the human beings of planet Earth, are not solely a physical entity, but also <u>necessarily possess</u> a *non-material* <u>inner animating core</u>: *For the physical cannot* – *and therefore* **does not** – *<u>animate</u> the physical!*

— — and — —

Crucial Imperative No 3:

That being more than just a physical body means we naturally and *inherently* possess a *<u>separable entity</u>* ***within*** the material form. And that *<u>that</u>* is the *actual* life-force, the *animating* core, that is *actually <u>each individual</u>!*

— will earth-science ever begin to finally complete their millions of text-books that, in the final analysis *without* the immutable and inviolable knowledge of **Creation-Law**, really only just ask more questions. The classic case of: **"The Error of Scientism!"** Pope Benedict XVI has correctly called to science to think differently:

> "Modern *scientific reason* quite simply has to accept the rational structure of matter and the correspondence *between our spirit* and the *prevailing* rational structures of nature *as a given*, on which its methodology *has to be based*. Yet the question why this has to be so, is a *real* question, and one which has to be remanded by the natural sciences *to other modes and planes of thought* – to **philosophy and theology**."

Notwithstanding that clear rationale from a greatly respected academic, the very *language* of the *dominating intellectual-educational authorities* of the many diverse countries, societies and cultures across the globe will surely *cry out **against*** the immutable **Creation-Law Truths** herein! So the final excision to bring to an end humankind's ongoing hereditary production of *aspiritual poison* will thankfully be forced upon us.

Isaiah, the Great Prophet, in **language** *powerfully-resonating* with **Spiritual Truth** and **Law**, warningly proclaims to humanity of this present era precisely what *we* also have been directed to explain. In this case – and thereby powerfully assisting *our* Mandate – we will, very thankfully, let the great Prophet and Servant of **The Creator** speak once more:

> "The 'Earth' also is ***defiled*** under the ***inhabitants*** thereof; because ***they*** have
> <u>***transgressed***</u> the Laws,
> <u>***changed***</u> the decrees,
> <u>***broken***</u> the everlasting covenant.
> Therefore has the ***curse*** devoured the 'Earth', and those that dwell therein ***are desolate***:...."
>
> (Isaiah 24:5-6, Fenton.
Emphases mine.)

Very much later Isaiah's dire warning for humankind was more strongly stated by One Who possessed the Absolute Mandate to so Proclaim. Since an exponential factor can be readily observed in all events now, the answer of Jesus to His Disciples when asked what the future-time [our time] would be like, is chilling.

> "...for there shall then be ***wide-spread affliction***, such as has ***not been known*** since the beginning of the world ***until now***, no, nor will ***ever*** be known again. And if those times were ***not*** cut short, ***not a man would be saved***".
>
> (Matthew 24:21-22, Fenton.
Emphases mine.)

0.4.7 Sexual Orientation and Creation-Law.

Sexual orientation: Personal choice – or other? Homosexuality and lesbianism: Natural – or an aberration? Do these practices transgress Isaiah's serious warning to humankind? And do they therefore *contribute* to now clearly imminent **"Global Societal Collapse"**; or do they not? What does **THE LAW** say?

As a general rule among probably *most peoples* historically, anything outside the man/woman union within societies was, for the most part, regarded as unacceptable. Thus running the gamut from undesirable, to offensive, to anathema. In some societies even to this day, punishable by death. Moreover, many cultures regarded – and still regard – the fertile woman as a blessing. When high infant mortality rates were once the norm in all societies, *producing-unions* maintained the numbers necessary for a society to be sufficiently viable for just simple survival to begin with; and for expansion and self-protection as a necessary adjunct.

So what has changed today? Whilst there have always been cultures where non-heterosexual preferences were tolerated, accepted, even embraced, the attitude and rulings of the Christian Church, in this area, primarily shaped the overall ethos of Western Nations. Notwithstanding changing societal attitudes and government-enacted legislation to legalise 'civil unions' for 'other kinds of relationships', the prevailing sentiment is still more one of non-acceptance to anything outside the man/woman paradigm.

In a truly strange and curious twist, however, the Teachings of Jesus are often used to justify *both sides* of the debate/clash, even from the pulpits of *opposing* ministers. Perhaps this *aberration* of *irreconcilable-divergence* stems from two *very different* interpretations of the so-called Christian-love ethos.

The *incorrect belief* that Jesus died to cleanse all human beings of their evil dispositions [i.e., *everyone's sins*] in His 'great act of Love' is seemingly the basis for an 'all-forgiving' attitude among some Christians towards virtually everything. For it *ostensibly* seeks to 'emulate' that 'loving sacrifice' in the Churches' interpretation of so-called 'Christian love' and forgive even serious transgressions, sometimes against the very Law Itself. Whilst there should ultimately be forgiveness – tempered by compassion of course – *true justice* must still nevertheless prevail.

In the final analysis, however, what is mooted as love is anything but, because it invariably fails to take into account **Justice**. **Creation-Law** *absolutely decrees* that **Love** and **Justice** cannot be separated. **They are one!** So where one is used without the other, **The Law of Balance** [explained further on] is then seriously transgressed.

Love: A small word, but one that has inadvertently caused so many problems due to the wrongful application of it in the unfortunate belief that it was always correctly applied. Because of its spiritually weak, earthly interpretation, we might designate the overall concept inherent in it as being almost a 'religion of earthly love'. For it is one thing to reverentially proclaim a belief in this power of love, but another to then apply it so wrongly that its distorted application produces the worst kinds of injustices. We need to therefore understand that **The Love of The Divine**, which produced the incomprehensible vastness of the physical universes – thus permitting us our material home – is actually severe, objective and impartial in its outworking. And therefore cannot possibly be equated with the weak, emotional, earthly caricature that we have produced in the *human* rendition of the word *love*.

For the moment putting aside non-heterosexual considerations: Perhaps the best kind of example to illustrate this premise is in the area of personal relationships, particularly in the search for a marriage partner. The emotional damage wrought largely by Hollywood's image-makers, coupled with the belief that pre-marital sex is necessary to determine whether two people will be 'suited' to a life together, has generated the ludicrous and almost farcical situation where 'shopping around to sample the goods' is believed to hold the key to a 'perfect marriage of true love'. Basically, in such situations, the concept of love is therewith reduced to the idea that it must surely be present in the intense feelings and emotions experienced with the 'best sexual partner'. Whilst such an encounter may certainly provide very powerful feelings of intense emotion, acceptance, and feeling good about oneself and that partner, it is not likely to be *true love*.[14]

In any case, if all such experimentation actually produced true love, we would surely not have the current, high divorce rate of the West.[15] Moreover, one would never know whether the *next* potential partner would be 'better' than the 'present *true* love'. This current societal attitude promotes views such as that recommended by Kathleen Quinlivan, a Canterbury University [New Zealand] sexual researcher who proposed that students:

> "...regardless of their sexual orientation...", should be allowed "...to explore a range of sexual identities and their implications."

One would have thought that any individual would have the free-will right to do so in any case. One does not need a University graduate to state a fundamental personal right to experiment and make a particular choice.

In her view it was important to recognise:

> "...the diversity and differences which existed within communities..." which would benefit "...gay, lesbian, bisexual and heterosexual youth alike."

---

[14]Interestingly, evidence suggests that in more simple and basic societies where "arranged marriages" are the norm, there appears to be a higher level of marriage fidelity, faithfulness and loyalty than that present in our so-called sophisticated, western cultures. Perhaps the key word here is responsibility, with duty as a close adjunct. We do not, however, advocate the 'arranged marriage' as the perfect solution, for personal *free will* should *always* determine the choice of a partner.

[15]Notwithstanding the societal stability that long-term marriages offer, we should nevertheless understand that some unions are meant for a particular time only. When such a union has run its ordained course, there is little to be gained in 'forcing' a continuation of it.

What is interesting in this case is that such views pressurise youth into possibly believing that the average boy/girl relationship – which, by the way, is the only kind that will *naturally* produce offspring – might somehow be unsound. And that the impressionable young must therefore be able to 'chop and change' to suit prevailing 'liberating expectations'. The ultimate horror in the present climate of inane 'political correctness' is, of course, to be labelled homophobic or something similar.
Reverend Gerald Hadlow, an Anglican minister, [New Zealand] on precisely this subject succinctly stated a necessary hope:
"Perhaps one day our youth will rediscover love, commitment."

From the standpoint of **Creation-Law**, we are not *the least bit interested* with any individual's personal choice – *in anything*! What we state here is that the inviolable outworking of **The Spiritual Laws** is absolute – *for every decision made*.

For the *purposes* of *this* particular discussion, then: **If** The Laws contained in The Bible, for example, *are* absolute, then the *kinds of advice* promoted by Kathleen Quinlivan for young people to 'liberate' themselves *from* the *so-called* 'debilitating constraints of homophobic views' are, in reality, nothing more than an advocacy of unnecessary and potentially dangerous experimentation. It is a view driven by the foolish emotionalism contained in the current global 'my rights' mindset. Why?

> Because under the *ultimate and non-negotiable* parameters of **Creation-Law**, any actual *'debilitating constraint'* is, *by extension*, then **actually present** in all so-called 'liberating sexual practices'. And therefore also in sexual orientation preferences *different* to that which **The Eternal Laws** decree as being *spiritually correct*.

So the actual *'debilitating constraint'* here is brought about simply by shackling oneself *to completely incorrect beliefs*.

In any case what social scientists determine for themselves and Western societies is rendered totally *irrelevant* by the sacrosanct nature of **Creation-Law**! For whatever choices we make *will bring* the reciprocal return; *without fail*. That is the inviolable outworking of **The Law of Reciprocal Action** operating in the lives of each of us. Therefore, the belief that one can somehow become *spiritually-liberated* by choosing a sexual preference which *does not* encompass the man/woman union is, in a word, **wrong**! Whilst our explanations may not fit at all with present societal mores, it is nevertheless especially important for young people to know that the age-old boy/girl relationship which brings more boys and girls onto the earth, is not only *perfectly okay*, but unequivocally derives from **The Eternal Laws!**

For any human being to *deny* the very obvious fact that the physical form of woman **perfectly complements** the physical form of man in a **natural union of intimacy** is laughable. For the two forms provide the *only* natural connection possible. Therefore, *despite* what the very loud global minority promote as being *natural*, any and every other intimate union of human beings in their physical forms is, by definition, naturally **unnatural**. That is not to say that such unions may be deemed politically and socially *acceptable* in the various cultures and societies of the world, but that is an entirely different matter.

Our purpose here is to elucidate **Creation-Law**; which *decrees/commands* only *naturalness* throughout Creation – especially and including **The World of Matter** and its *inhabitants*. All else – which can only come into existence via the free-will volition of we human beings in any case – **must**, and **will**, be finally driven by the **Pressure** and **Power** of that very **Law** to its *demise*; a polite word in this case.

Liberal ideas such as we have examined in this overall segment, anchored primarily in the intellectually-derived 'Human Rights' mentality now solidly entrenched in mainstream Western thinking, have thus found their final end-excrescence enacted in the earthly legislative law of many countries. In 'earthly law' where 'voiced opposition' to such laws can, in certain circumstances, be *perversely deemed* an actual 'criminal' offence.

Dr Alan Duggan, an Australian researcher into Male Health, stated to an Auckland Unitec seminar that anecdotal evidence from studies carried out in Canada and Australia suggest that young male suicide statistics may lean as much as *30 per cent* to more suicides 'among homosexual men than straight men'. From that line of research alone, one can see that the higher suicide rate amongst this group does not indicate any kind of 'liberation' at all – rather the opposite. Dr Duggan opined that the research results pointed to a *'sexual orientation/identity crisis'* in this group.

Once again, and purely for the purposes of this discussion, *if*

"The Spiritual Laws of Creation" are not believed to be absolute or not believed to exist at all, then *disbelievers* should simply continue to live on in their *disbelief*, particularly of the effects of **The Law of Reciprocal Action** visiting any hard suffering upon them. In all cases under the aegis and increased power inherent in the "whirlwind constant".

> **Do not then, however, apportion blame elsewhere if personal decisions and desires should visit return effects *vastly different* to what one might have wished for – before the fact!**

In any case, it must eventually 'all come out in the wash' one way or the other. As previously stressed, The Spiritual Laws cannot be transgressed with impunity – either by any one person or any so-called *'liberated group'*.

From *our* free-will viewpoint, we really *are* all free to choose our particular likes, but we nonetheless affirm that those same decisions are most certainly *not* free of *the spiritual consequences*. Thus, whilst it is everyone's personal right to so choose, have the **courage** to then *accept* the reciprocal effect of those decisions and do not expect that all others must agree with, or even approve of, any particular choice of sexual orientation. Despite possible disapproval or even revulsion toward certain choices and/or practices, however, such choices nevertheless ultimately remain the preserve of the 'choosers' and should at least be *respected* as that by all others.

The Book of Leviticus provides interesting reading in this regard. One's personal views – or perhaps sexual orientation choice – would probably engender one of two reactions when examining this particular Book of The Bible; a strong or angry emotional one, or perhaps more relaxed acceptance. Regardless of individual views, however, and even though perhaps more addressing the Priesthood from the Tribe of Levi, 'Leviticus' nevertheless provides a valuable insight and guide for more correct *spiritual living* than current so-called 'liberating' views are probably prepared to accept.

For example, Verses 6-29 of Chapter 18 of **'Leviticus'** are sub-headed:

The Laws of Affinity, and Marriages and Sex.

The most interesting aspect of those twenty three Scriptural Verses [also Chapter 20:1-21] is the fact that they embody much of the cultural/social and moral foundation of *most* societies, cultures and religions globally. Why should that be so? Historically, why have non-Christian societies also regarded these kinds of 'Rules for Life' as fundamental for their social stability too? Alluded to or written about in other religious works, the detailed substance of the Sexual Laws in the face-book of the Christian religion – The Bible – quite simply supplies the spiritual and moral parameters for *correct* human living.

Copulation in the *manner* of a man and woman where it is actually *not so*, is therein labelled an **abomination**. In the present climate of 'anything goes", such *words* are mostly regarded as just irksome *religious irrelevance*. However, under the *inviolable* outworking of **The Creation Laws of Life**, *absolutely relevant* and ultimately **death-dealing** in the *second* sense.[16]

> The *natural* human/societal *repugnance* toward sexual involvement in practices such as paedophilia, incest and bestiality etc., clearly reveal that *abhorrence to activities which encompass the immoral and unnatural* is therefore *fundamentally inherent* in the psyche or spirit of human beings. Thus, to stand *outside* that 'inherent compass' means exactly that.

With regard to current views, we can perhaps describe modern man's general interpretation of love as little more than 'emotional self-indulgence' which, when ostensibly expressing love toward another, too often means: **'I want *you* to love me!'**

However, if the foundation for a union is a *genuine* spiritual bond in the first instance, then we may more safely say that *true love* is probably present. Within such a partnership, moreover, all other factors – including that of sexual intimacy – will invariably be emotionally and physically fulfilling also. And because the correct foundation of **The Spiritual** was striven for first as the most important part of the union, it will naturally have the greatest *potential* to be an harmonious one too.

Therefore genuine love will always be concerned with what **spiritually benefits** the other, and not necessarily with what might be personally gratifying or agreeable to him. Thus, the latter-day concept of 'tough love' for wayward teenagers owes its relative success to the fact that its 'genesis' is anchored in the Justice of **Spiritual Law**.

---

[16]Fully explained in the Chapter: "The Second Death" in the Parent Work.

Because the application of the word, love, mirrors a lack of *true* understanding of the meaning of it as contained within The Spiritual Laws, the admonition to "Love thy neighbour" and "Love your enemies" does not mean *giving them what they want* or what pleases them. It means only doing for them that which will benefit them *spiritually*. If it means possible hardship from *their* personal point of view, then that may actually be the correct kind of *love*. Otherwise how else can they learn, or grow?

To that end the spiritual explanations contained in this Booklet elucidates and expresses that 'new concept' in its necessary severity, thus offering Love and Justice in Spiritual Knowledge!

We of global humanity must therefore find the strength to apply the concept of *love* in the right way – if we wish to live spiritually-correctly. This means that even *family* members should not demand what others may have worked hard for under an emotional-blackmail mode in a totally wrong and selfish use of the word. Misplaced indulgence would mean the continuation of the same faults in the *generations* and, by subsequent extension, holding them within the various races. The end result is that *everyone* continues to slide *further* on the *downward* path. That would not be displaying love. On the contrary, by acting thus one would place oneself in the position of not acting spiritually-correctly toward a fellow human being, even if of the *same race or family*. This different and radical view contrasts greatly with what we have too readily accepted thus far as 'true love'.

So where does this kind of 'love' fit in societies seeking respite from constantly deteriorating standards and morals – let alone just the increasing struggles of everyday life in the glaringly-obvious reality of **"Global Societal Collapse"** *across the board.*

For some Christians and Christian groups, their particular brand of 'Jesus-love' sanctifies homosexuality and lesbianism because – according to this belief – all practices where so-called 'love' is present must be natural and thus in concert with 'genuine' Christian principles. With regard to the weak, Christian application of the word, love, we should note that Jesus, Himself, as a manual worker under Joseph the carpenter, would have been *physically strong* in the first instance. The fact that He was also obviously Spiritually-Powerful and not weak and vacillating, is clearly illustrated in the New Testament in His very severe admonitions to many people, *particularly to men of intellect*. His admonition to:

> "Go and do thou likewise!"

– is clear testimony to His 'Loving severity' toward humankind. We should therefore regard 'love' as a very real and consistent 'power' in which there will be found no weakness, or illogical or emotional indulgence. We must learn to emulate Jesus, the personification of Divine Love, in His 'Loving severity'!

Thus: Love is a <u>Power</u>, not an emotion!

Wherever it is applied, every application of the word, *love* must carry the same connotation if we wish to at least *ameliorate some aspects* of the nonetheless *now unstoppable* "**Global Societal Collapse**". Such is the immutable, and unstoppable, outworking of **The Law of Reciprocal Action** –

0.5 The Law of Spiritual Gravity!

0.5.1 Gravity! – The Spiritual Dynamic.

In accordance with *Newton's* "Law on Universal Gravitation", the idea of a force of gravity is readily understandable in the physical sense of the word. Quite logically, heavy objects fall to the ground whilst very light substances may rise. So the effect we see materially is the form by which this Law, **The Law of Spiritual Gravity**, manifests on earth.

The everyday unconscious outworking of the effect of "The Law of Gravity" is revealed in earthly sayings that reflect this concept in society as a whole. However, whilst the effect of this particular Law clearly displays obvious physical characteristics, it is first and foremost a Spiritual one. For instance, we often speak of "heavy thoughts" and "light thoughts", or the effect that a "heavy person" may have upon us as opposed to the much more enjoyable company of a "light person". Evil thoughts and practices are rightly recognised as being of a "heavy nature", whilst noble thoughts and deeds are similarly accepted as occupying a far higher level.

Thus the same gravitational effect that takes place in a physical setting also occurs in a non-physical environment. It is one, moreover, which impacts very decisively on the fate of man *after* his earthly demise! That is because the actual person or individual is more than just a heavy physical body. Our true self, or actual conscious personality, is that of our inner animating core – our spirit. **That is who and what we actually are.**

At earthly death, therefore, we simply discard, or step out of, the physical form that all human beings are obliged to take upon entry onto the earth plane. This shell, our overcoat, is then subject to the natural processes of decay and disintegration in accordance with The Laws of Nature, which is the *earthly outworking* of The Spiritual Laws of Creation. This completely natural process thus allows the soul body, which consists of a number of non-physical bodies enveloping the spirit, to become free of its previously heavy "garment". However, it is not then able to go wherever it wishes, for this process is determined by The Law of Spiritual Gravity acting upon all the "works" connected to each individual. Thus the Biblical warning: *"Their works shall follow them."*

Base propensities and activities whilst in the physical body on earth weigh the *coverings* of the spirit down causing it to sink, to fall away in a direction opposite to its true origin in the Spiritual Realm. Thus the entity regresses. The depth to which it sinks is strictly determined by the extent to which it indulged in wrong-doing that, in turn, gives it its corresponding "spiritual weight" or heaviness. The particular level to which it sinks will be peopled by those with similar base propensities or weaknesses, in accordance with The Law of Attraction of Similar Species.

It is important to understand that under the Eternal Laws **only here on Earth can good and evil live side by side**. Every other Plane of Creation is formed according to its comparative "weight" – lightest and purest at the top, and heaviest and darkest at the bottom. In this lies the most wonderful justice because each individual spirit automatically ends up in the plane corresponding to its personal volition, thereby automatically receiving **what it strove for most**.

If a recently departed spirit has lived a life of, say, lust and greed for example – a very good illustration given the deplorable state of humankind today – it will be drawn to the same level as others similar to it. In such an environment similar souls will give full vent to their propensity for lust and greed upon each other continuously. This same happening will be repeated in other places at other levels where the propensities for violence, drunkenness, nicotine and drug addiction, gluttony, laziness, and anger etc., hold sway. There, in situations as depraved and potentially as hopeless as that described, is the place we call "hell".

Yes, **hell is *we* have created** but need not, and should not, **ever have done so.**

Yet even there the Eternal Laws, which also automatically incorporate Divine Love, are ever watchful for souls who, through inner recognition, finally become disgusted with themselves and their tormented environment and petition for their release from it. With this personal awakening to the truth of their situation and the longing to be free of it, a way is automatically opened for such souls to begin their ascent to the next higher level.

Through their awakening to personal recognition and desire for change, they would have become different in nature to their particular environment, thereby ensuring an automatic separation from it in accordance with The Spiritual Laws – notably: "The Law of Attraction of Similar Species" and "The Law of Gravity" under the outworking of "The Law of Movement". (Note: "The Law of Attraction..." is, inherently, also a "law of repulsion".) Thus any soul can ascend, even out of such grievous circumstances, if its desire to do so is sufficiently strong.

Contrast that situation with one where a soul has striven to do noble deeds all its earth life; where it had sought to find Spiritual Truth; where it had offered compassion and kindness; where its thoughts and aspirations had sought elevation. Such a life makes a spirit light and buoyant. Upon shedding its physical shell at earthly death, its spiritual lightness draws it upwards toward Planes of Light. There it will find spirits who exhibit the same kinds of noble traits it had developed. Whereas the inhabitants of the lower regions are surrounded by their own base volition, those in the higher planes of Light experience the living reality of the greater contentment and happiness synonymous with striving for more noble aspirations. Thus, Perfect Justice!

For those who *choose to believe* that spiritual ascent lies **solely** in a belief of faith in Jesus, consider His severe words. From Matthew 5:18 and 5:26. [Emphases mine.]

> "...that until the heavens and the earth shall pass away, a single dot or hairstroke shall not disappear from the law, until **all has been completed**."

> "I tell you indeed, that you will not depart until **you** have **repaid the very last farthing**."

The Law of Spiritual Gravity has logically existed since time immemorial, yet it is interesting to note that Newton's theories and discoveries in the earthly environment paved the way for a rapid increase in knowledge of astronomy and allowed for further interstellar discoveries. Moreover, the simplicity of The Laws that hold the moon in stable orbit around the earth without either crashing into it through its stronger gravitational pull, or simply heading off into space, convinced Newton that only *"a few natural laws apply to the whole universe"*.

He demonstrated that The Laws which govern the planets of our solar system's elliptical paths around the sun, are the same Laws that also govern all moving bodies, and therefore apply everywhere in the entire universe. Notwithstanding the Hermetic adage of "as in heaven, so on earth", his radical view of the time generally put to rest a conflicting belief that there is "one set of laws for heaven and another here on earth". Because Newton believed that the same natural laws applied everywhere in the universe, this would clearly have posed a potential "crisis of faith" for any Orthodox Church view of God. Newton's own faith, however, was never shaken. On the contrary, he regarded the natural laws **as *proof* of the *existence* of a great and Almighty God.**

0.6 The Law of Balance!

0.6.1 Balance in Life! – A Vital Necessity.

> "Virtue, then, is a disposition involving choice. It consists of a mean, relative to us, defined by reason and as the reasonable man would define it. It is a mean between two vices – one of excess, the other of deficiency."
>
> (Aristotle, 384-322 BC, from Nichomachaen Ethics, Bk. 2)

Had Aristotle lived today he would probably be horrified at the excesses relating to such things as extremes of wealth, and in personal body-development. In his view these kinds of activities and practices were just as unbalanced as someone who only uses his head. He considered such extremes to be an expression of a warped way of life. Aristotle also applied the "Golden Mean" to human relationships. He believed that we must be neither cowardly nor rash, but courageous (too little courage is cowardice, too much is rashness), neither miserly nor extravagant but liberal (not liberal enough is miserly, too liberal is extravagant). The same applied to eating. He thought it was dangerous to eat too little, but also dangerous to eat too much. The ethics of both Plato and Aristotle contain echoes of Greek medicine. **The Law of Balance**, in its perfect outworking, is Aristotle's "Golden Mean".

Aristotle believed that for some acts there is no mean at all; their very nature already implies badness, such as spite, envy, adultery, theft, and murder. These are bad in themselves and not in their excesses and deficiencies. One is always wrong in doing them. (Philosophy History & Problems, Samuel Enoch Stumpf, p 99.) Achieving a happy or "harmonious" life, therefore, can only be attained by exercising balance in temperament.

Generally regarded as probably the first philosopher/scientist, Aristotle divided everything in the natural world into two main categories. In one corner he placed what he termed the non-living things such as rocks, clumps of soil and drops of water etc., and in the other the classification of "living things". He further divided this latter group into two other categories: "plants" and the "other creatures". This last was finally divided into two sub-categories: animals and humans.

Aristotle further reasoned that the "form" of man comprised three parts; a plant-like part, an animal part and a rational part (the soul or "divine reason"). In his view, man could only live a good life and achieve happiness by using all his abilities and capabilities. In the three forms of happiness that he identified, the first was a life of pleasure and enjoyment, the second as a free and responsible citizen, and the third as a thinker and philosopher. All three needed to be present at the same time for happiness to be attained within the individual, for he rejected all forms of *imbalance*. Thus, The Law of Balance was well understood in those early years.

In Spiritual terms this Law, in its effect and outworking, should reflect the necessary *balance* between "giving" and "receiving". In everyday tasks, many even mundane things automatically obey this law. Like a baby taking its first faltering steps, or a young child learning to stay upright on a bicycle, waiters balancing plates of food in cafes, or even the simple act of walking. On construction sites we observe large cranes with enormous working booms counter-balanced by opposing shorter boom lengths appropriately counter-weighted to achieve safe working balances. The activities of trade and monetary transaction may require the use of scales for various purposes. In many judicial systems, justice is depicted by a set of scales held by a blindfolded woman, traditionally meaning "Justice is blind". Perhaps, however, reflecting the wish that a correct weighing and examining in the Courts might be the outcome, for if there is no balance where lies justice? Justice should not be blind, however, but *all-seeing and spiritually discerning*.

The simplest and most quietly obvious example of The Law of Balance is in breathing. We must naturally balance exhaling with inhaling. Correct breathing is vital for optimum health, but shallow breathing into the top of the lungs only does not provide this. The solution in this case is to regard the "outbreath" as the key. Exhaling properly and emptying the lungs will automatically ensure that a full breath will next be inhaled. Many a respiratory disorder can be at least relieved with consistent and correctly-balanced breathing.

In the home and in the nation, the need to balance the budget is important in order to live within our means. The daily intake of food generally indicates a basic understanding of the need to try to achieve a "balanced diet" for optimum health i.e., different kinds of foods in appropriate proportions. Quite obviously, too much of just one type of food is not only inappropriate and tiresome, but is also not beneficial for the normal digestive system. Balancing the necessary intake of food is the need to eliminate body wastes as a natural result of this process. Any imbalance resulting from poor digestion or constipation makes us feel unwell.

Workaholic burnout as a result of "all work and no play" is also a transgression against The Law of Balance. Conversely, a life characterised by no work is equally harmful, even after retirement. The right kind of work for each individual should be a feature of the retirement years to help maintain the health of the body until death. Where the elderly happily engage in appropriate activity, higher levels of health are achieved. And where job opportunities are not readily available for someone wishing to work, low self-esteem may be the outcome resulting in a decline in the emotional and physical health of that individual.

The Laws of Creation show us that they inherently possess Divine Love. Love is thus the greatest Power. Also inherent in this as a part of Divine Love is Perfect Justice. The two cannot be separated. The Law of Balance, under the aegis of the power of Love and Spiritual Justice, ensures that *everlasting rest* is not the reality of the after-death situation. No one *rests in peace*! That particular concept/belief must surely rate as one of the strangest of human "inventions". We are **compelled** to accept the responsibility of our life's decisions and **live them out**, so to speak, even after our physical demise. Then, our "personal books" are audited to determine where there is imbalance, after which we must spiritually address it, i.e., put it right!

If more people recognised this stark reality – which cannot be circumvented in any case – there might arise a better attitude to many things, since earthly death is the "great leveller" for all. A knowledge of The Law of Balance would therefore certainly benefit the elderly, and those consciously approaching death through illness or accident etc.. Perhaps a greater effort might then be placed on "balancing one's spiritual account" long before being *overtaken* by earthly death.

Unfortunately, however, our present way of thinking clearly shows a general propensity for two things:

1. to seek as much wealth in the shortest possible time.

2. for a life of ease ever after on earth.

Great wealth can achieve wonderful goals and is not, in itself, a bad thing. However, if it is used for base, superficial or selfish ends it loses its great potential and value and spiritually degrades the holder/s of it. It is a sad indictment on today's society that spiritual goals or earthly activities with a spiritual content are not regarded or valued highly as befits their true worth. The scales of society are well and truly tipped toward overindulgence, base passions and immorality, to our spiritual detriment.

Benjamin Franklin (1706-90) observed that if there were no limiting factors in nature, one species of plant or animal could engulf the entire globe. The balance is maintained because many species hold each other in check. Man is the only "spanner in the works" here, as his activities invariably create imbalance.

In what is arguably the most difficult yet necessary part of the everyday life of the human spirit i.e., that of personal relationships, the correct application of The Law of Balance between "giving and taking" offers the key to harmony and progress in all situations. Whether in marriage between partners, in a family situation between parents and children, between employer and employee, or between groups or nations; in each particular case the concept of giving and taking needs to be correctly understood.

Parents desiring to have children must be aware of the need to balance this with the duty to care for the child in the right way.[17] Where parents offer spiritually-correct protection and nurturing to their children, this must be balanced by the obligation of the

---

[17]The huge rise in child abuse and paedophilia, even in family groups, clearly attests to terribly imbalanced and sick societies.

offspring to then respect their parents, but only where parents or care-givers have *earned the right* to be respected, of course. For why should parents be *automatically honoured* by offspring if they are not deserving of honour?

The ostensibly sacrosanct Commandment – "**Honour Thy Father and Mother**" – should be very carefully thought about as to its *correct* meaning. Societal statistics clearly reveal the fact that many parents are not worthy to be honoured in any way at all by their children. Violence, drunkenness, drug-taking, abuse etc., can never be raised as the kinds of examples and behaviour for children to be exposed to, and certainly not to aspire to. Even though individual souls are brought together in family groups under the precise and lawful outworking of Spiritual Law, it still behoves parents to live - and thus teach by example – the correct Spiritual principles of life.

We should understand, therefore, that this Commandment was given *first and foremost for parents!* It was, in the very first instance, for parents to *honour* the concept and duty of **Fatherhood and Motherhood**. So that they *would* become such parents as *could* be honoured by their children. For it was surely not the children born to their union who made the decision for their parents. In the light of Perfect Love and Perfect Justice, it is *absolutely inconceivable* that the Perfection of The Creator would *Command* children to honour parents who had no right to be honoured. That is the true meaning of this Commandment; that parents live correctly according to the Law, and thereby *imbue* the status of parenthood *with honour!*.

Yet, for one or two Churches, the "letter of the law" is so strictly enforced that some family groups within them live not in love and harmony, but in fear. We may therefore wonder how many children, raised by strictly religious parents who, themselves, did not obey the Commandments or live correctly, yet nevertheless still hypocritically demanded that they be honoured. I am sure that many a child or young adult has suffered greatly under this kind of arrogant and hypocritical religious injustice.

Once the child has reached an age where it is physically able to assist in the home, it should be required to do so in order to balance the parental care it receives. Its form of assistance would be commensurate with its age and abilities. A child brought up *without* the application of this Law in its life may not develop any kind of purposeful work ethic, nor garner the correct social skills and attitude necessary to interact in a naturally balanced way with others. An attitude of personal selfishness is often the outcome that, unfortunately, may become ingrained for life. The spiritually correct concept of "tough love" for wayward children today might not have been needed for many had The Law of Balance been applied from the outset.

It should not be assumed, however, that the overall application of that Law must necessarily require a *similar* kind of return contribution or payment to that received. Personal circumstances may decree otherwise. In such cases the recipient will fulfil the requirements of this Law if he evinces deep and genuine gratitude for the help received. Or perhaps he may be able to tender good advice to his benefactor who may well be able to put to good use for himself. So, regardless of personal situations, everyone is able to fulfil the demands of The Law of Balance in some way. The fact that many do not do so stands as a reflection of our level of spiritual immaturity where the unhelpful human traits of selfishness, thoughtlessness, or just plain bad habits have become more the norm.

Thus, in respecting this Law, we should not unnecessarily worry about what should be given in return. It behoves us to simply give the best of what we have and what we can, *relative* to what was received and what we are *able* to give. If this should mean genuine thanks only, without guile or deceit, then the demands of the Law are fulfilled. Legal contracts are not included here, that is a different matter. Everybody, rich or poor, is therefore able to *live* this most necessary Law. Even the poorest can give out of themselves gratitude, a heartfelt prayer, or even a kind look to the giver. So long as the heart is pure and the intention genuine, the essential considerations from the standpoint of The Spiritual Laws will have been fulfilled.

The outworking of The Law of Balance in the present time can be powerfully observed in a specific problem area now coming to acute prominence. Mankind's questing nature and technological drive guaranteed that he would journey to and explore lands far from his birthplace. And, of course, colonise and settle some of them. Major wars have also been a driving force for people to flee to nearby safer areas, and perhaps settle there. Prior to the Age of Exploration such "refugee movements" were generally confined to the continent of Europe. Because the population numbers were not high, the "resettling" impact could be absorbed much more easily than is the case today.

During the Industrial Revolution, however, the situation changed dramatically. The industrialised nations – of which many were the main maritime ones also – shipped into their burgeoning economies thousands and thousands of workers from other places around the globe. Some went voluntarily, others were enslaved. Whilst it made some nations and individuals very wealthy, the balance of the world's peoples was, from then on, more drastically altered than at any time before. The huge dislocation caused by the Second World War compounded the problem considerably.

With a global population now at the seven billion mark and increasing rapidly, and more people seeking a so-called "better life" in lands sometimes at an opposite end of the globe, the huge and fundamental imbalance in the ethnic mix of peoples in the different countries of the world that began in earnest just a few centuries ago has now become like a "sword of Damocles" hanging over many countries of the more wealthy West. That unfortunate legacy has produced desperate acts of violence, political instability, social unrest and urban terrorism on a previously unknown and frightening scale. It has now resulted in demands for stronger measures to curb immigration in the refugee crisis of the present day.

The ostensibly compassionate practice of Western Nations accepting refugees from parts of the world where unstable, corrupt or oppressive regimes hold sway does not *ultimately* solve the problem for the people of the country concerned. *They, themselves, should strive to bring about correct change within.* Unfortunately, however, external influences often undermine well-intentioned efforts to influence such change. Dubious foreign policy objectives of some Western Governments, big business dealings, UN mandated operations and badly monitored aid programs have all contributed to abuse, corruption and incredible suffering for millions.

It is precisely this kind of aspiritual, greedy and ignoble behaviour that has driven much of the refugee problem. It is not our purpose to analyse the global situation of the why of refugees to any depth here. The world's news and refugee agencies do an admirable job in highlighting these problems; and constantly supply a surfeit of visual images.

What we unequivocally state, however, is that these kinds of problems, *as with all others*, have their origin in mankind ignoring the very Laws that drive and govern all outcomes from every decision made.

Thus we note the clear and unequivocal fact that the world, its peoples, its systems, its religions etc., are in serious and dangerous imbalance. For not one thing, not one decision, stands alone in the world. All are ultimately connected. Because they *are* all in some way connected, a decision in one part of the world produces a ripple effect in every other – even if not perceived immediately or at all. This lawful effect can thus be seen developing *more and more strongly* in the international and religious tensions now surfacing over refugees and immigration.

Desperation and riots, people smuggling, religious and ethnic tensions and hatred; these extreme outcomes simply reveal the emerging end-effect of this particular outworking under the aegis of The Law of Balance. It places increasingly stronger spiritual pressure on all of humanity to recognise and understand why there is so much conflict in a practice that "seemingly" seeks to *help* the downtrodden. That in itself is a noble and correct ideal of course, and forever will remain so. If not applied and effected spiritually-correctly, however, then disaster will be the end-result. That is the path we currently tread. There may well be a place for refugee assistance into other countries, **but the reason must be a spiritually correct one in the first instance.**

The refugee group and the Government accepting the entry of that group to their country should fully understand the import of such a decision. For The Law of Balance will *ultimately redress imbalance* wherever it occurs, irrespective of the reasons for the original decision. In the case of latter-day pressures to accept refugee quotas, The Law of Balance does not mean *equal* balance in ethnic numbers, it is more about the *balance of harmony* – for that country and that society and culture. Refugee groups that refuse to integrate in an harmonious way should perhaps consider whether they should have remained in the country of their ethnic origin after all.

The various peoples and cultures of the world **are meant to be different and diverse.** Those essential differences, however, are obviously most powerfully reflected and *harmonised for the benefit of all peoples of the world* in and through the "beauty of the peoples and cultures" *within the borders of the lands that represent and actually are of that people.* Of course we all understand that movement and settlement into other lands to seek a better life or freedom from oppression or persecution is a natural aspect of humanity. And without those sorts of motivational considerations, many millions of the world's peoples would not now be generationally-settled into countries far removed from ancestral homelands.

The increasing and strident racist vitriol we now hear from so many quarters we now hear may not be so much racist but more a sub-conscious knowing that *so much* ethnic resettlement over such a relatively *short period* has not permitted sufficient time for *normal and natural assimilation* as was the situation previously. In any case, there are no solutions or answers in the same old arguments that each "side" – the pro's and the anti's – continue to push. Because the problem now virtually feeds on itself, the only alternative insight that *might* have *once* brought order out of increasing chaos is probably no longer viable. Therefore, in accordance with the mandated purpose of this work, we unequivocally state that the posturing and bluster of politicians and concerned individuals and groups worldwide for increasing refugee quotas into so-called "better" countries, will fail without the correct "Spiritual" insight.

Equally for those individuals and groups who stand in opposition; they, too, must take into account the essential knowledge of Spiritual Law if they are to correctly understand the true nature of what is currently fermenting to its final conclusion. Spiritual knowledge and concomitant application of it by both groups – the authorities on the one hand and the supplicants on the other – would have provided the only real solution. It is unlikely that that will be the outcome anywhere now. The Law of Balance has been transgressed very seriously for a long time now. Therefore, *balance **will** be restored equally seriously,* **but in a much shorter time period!**

0.6.2 To Give, or to Take?

"It is more blessed to give than to receive!" (Acts 20:35, Fenton.)

These words of Jesus, like many of them, have been so misunderstood or so grossly misinterpreted that it has become difficult to fulfil His words of the Law in the way He originally taught them, even with the very best of intentions. Yet the question of whether one should give or take is readily answered in the understanding that in The Law of Balance between giving and taking, *giving* always ranks first. Unfortunately, through the well-intentioned but misplaced "generosity" of some social groups and churches, "taking" as a "social right" has become a way of life for some people and families who have no idea that they should also **give** *something* in return.

Whether intentional or not, this transgression of The Law of Balance has a detrimental effect on the one who is a constant receiver, not least to the individual's self-esteem and self-respect.

Moreover, children raised in this environment may become unwitting transgressors of this Law later in their life, also to their detriment. Thus, through a lack of understanding of an Eternal Law, well-meaning people can actually perpetuate and enlarge a social problem as their good intent, in certain cases, does not always translate to giving the correct and necessary kind of "Spiritual" and material help actually needed.

A thorough knowledge of The Spiritual Laws is the only way that humanity can address its increasing social problems. In determining the best way that we might offer help, we should always be cognisant of the ancient Asian saying:

> " *"Give a man a fish, and you feed him for a day. Teach him to fish, and you feed him for life!"*

At the beginning of this Booklet we stated that each Law examined would intermesh with all the other Eternal Laws to produce a perfectly balanced whole, and that the reader should be able to perceive the connections between them all. In this case, and as a simple example, one can easily deduce that *giving* in the correct way is better because it is connected to the Law of Sowing and Reaping. The act of giving is identical with the practice of sowing. For each seed will, at its appropriate time, provide multiples of the same kinds of seeds for the *giver*.

Conversely, that which one extends the hand for – the seed taken or received – is like a harvest. Once consumed, it ceases to exist. With each receiving, a cycle is closed. Whenever we give, however, we start a new cycle. Through this process, therefore, it is always better to give than to receive. Of course, any giving should not be coloured solely by the selfish desire for a large return, thus losing sight of the correct spiritual reason to want to give in the first place. When viewed in this light, the words of Jesus take on a far deeper and richer meaning than might previously have been understood.

As we noted in the earlier sub-heading, **"Families and Children"**, the current social propensity to demand one's rights, whether individual, children's, youth, ethnic, cultural, social, legal, religious, or any other, in the first instance lives the aspect of "taking"! In the sense of The Spiritual Laws, it is a negative and selfish attitude, for rights are only obtained by the fulfilment of responsibilities or duties. Therefore, *the fulfilment of duty and responsibility must come before any claim to rights*. This vitally necessary attitude should be inculcated into every individual through education in the home, in the schools, in the collective workplaces, and perhaps more especially in the gaols.

Consider the effect on society if, instead of demanding more and more "rights", we all immediately and radically changed our way of thinking to encompass a new, more tolerant and giving attitude which saw us all become concerned with *responsibilities, duties and obligations*. Toward each other, between parents and children, teachers and students, employer and employee, between religions and ethnic groups, even between individuals within those ethnic groups, from the criminal to his victim, and the individual to society.

In one single stroke of "attitude", our present kind of oftentimes selfish society could be instantly transformed into one that actually lived the completely beneficial aspects of Spiritual Law, particularly that of "The Law of Sowing and Reaping". Virtually overnight, all manner of social problems and crime could disappear, and confrontation could also quickly become a distant memory; a memory of pointless, debilitating argument, anger and violence. Whilst this may seem an unworkable utopian ideal, nothing more than a pipe dream, it is exactly possible. In any case, without such a change the misguided "Human Rights first" ethos will continue to ensure that the current "my rights mantra" will simply further entrench a particular and insidious selfishness in society.

Thus one should give out of a genuine desire to help, and in the manner most *spiritually* beneficial to the recipient. The Eternal Laws therefore urge everyone to give, and no one should practice or indulge in one-sided taking. As previously stated, however, it would be wrong to expect any kind of *particular* return from the person to whom one has given, as the act of giving is then denigrated to an unspoken, selfish, strings-attached, silent demand – for something in return. In the strict lawfulness of this process, what should be recognised is that what might be received in return for what one has given does not necessarily depend upon the recipient. This may initially be a difficult concept to adjust to. Yet whether or not it is believed the recipient deserves it, whether or not he is grateful or ungrateful, and even whether or not he is actually aware that he has been helped, all such considerations are ultimately irrelevant. In any case ingratitude for any kindness shown will bring its own "reward" to the "ungrateful one".

It is a very human trait to seek recognition for any kind of help offered, yet the outworking of The Law of Reciprocal Action applies here equally as much as our attitude toward the suffering. What comes to us as our exact due – our reward as it were – arrives in the manner and at the time so ordained under The Spiritual Laws. Since we do not necessarily harvest in the same season that we sow, the time of its return may not be immediate. [18]

The same principles should apply whether the giver or receiver is an individual, a group, or a nation. Here, also, it is more blessed to give than to receive. Many developed nations give aid and technical assistance to others, and this serves to promote a large measure of peace, harmony and goodwill in the world. If every recipient nation were to give something in return, a wonderful system of dynamic exchange and interaction would emerge, thus promoting global development in the right way. Every recipient nation *can* give something in return, be it cultural exchanges, or only genuine gratitude and appreciation.

At this point it is timely to reiterate that under the increased spiritual pressure now pouring onto the earth and its inhabitants, all past imbalances will be forcibly, and therefore severely, corrected. In future, deviation from The Law of Balance will not be able to be sustained for as long as has been possible thus far. The present structural problems that can be observed in the national and global economies, in particular through failing banks and financial institutions, are a direct result of mankind's total disregard for, and lack of understanding of, The Law of Balance. The disruption inherent in the economic and social stress of major restructuring programmes world-wide is the result of the effect of this increased pressure now culminating in urgent attempts to restore balance where, previously, there was imbalance; even if it appeared *not* to be the case.

Therefore the first task of the restructuring agencies should be to ensure that the process is carried out for the right reasons and under the knowledge of this Law, with due regard for the respect and integrity of those duly affected. Restructuring purely for the sake of doing so, without clear reasons and goals, will only ensure unnecessary upheaval. So it behoves the architects of necessary change to become thoroughly conversant with the Eternal Laws, especially The Law of Balance, if they wish to succeed. Quite obviously, only those areas that actually *need* restructuring should be worked upon. Any area that is already in balance should be

---

[18] The immediacy of financial transactions are a different matter, concerned solely with business expectations and practices, unless perhaps fraud or deceit is planned.

left alone, whether in international trade, in the financial system including setting exchange rates, in the determination of prices for goods and services and in industrial relations.

Since most Company restructuring involves the down-sizing of work forces and their pay rates, with the generally greedy practice of those who institute the changes greatly increasing their own salary levels, it would be timely for such people to become cognisant of this Law, if only for their own spiritual growth. Otherwise their "greed", or their "works" will one day pursue *them*. For the Law takes no account of supposedly "sharp' business practices. In terms of the attitude of such "Boards of Directors" or "C.E.O's" to the workers who help produce the business profits for them, the correct application of this Law is well illustrated in the admonition attributed to Jesus:

"*...for the workman is entitled to his wages.*"

(Luke 10:7, Fenton.)

In the international arena, the practice of advancing huge loans to poorer, under-developed nations, and then expecting outrageously exorbitant interest charges from them, has been rightly likened to a blood transfusion – "*from a **sick** patient to a **healthy** one*". Where is there fairness and balance in such cases? To cite global monetary vagaries as the reason why cheap loans cannot be advanced from rich nations to poor, quite clearly shows that we should quickly set about bringing it into balance. Thankfully, a new idea is fermenting among some lenders. Any system that permits the electronic transfer of large currency amounts to reap huge profits simply because of a small shift in an exchange rate somewhere in the world is clearly obscene. Such practices should serve as a warning that this completely out-of-balance, globally-interconnected monetary system cannot be sustained, simply because the Spiritual pressure of The Law of Balance will one day bring about its collapse.

Interestingly, the December 1996 Edition of *Time* Magazine noted a subtle but growing shift in the attitude of *some* of the richest Americans. In the opinion of billionaire Ted Turner, the wish of the majority of those Americans to make *Forbes* magazine's listing of the 400 wealthiest, "...is destroying our country," claiming that the "ole skinflints" are so afraid of slipping down the *Forbes* list ... that they hoard, rather than share, their wealth."

"Turner issued a challenge: rank the biggest 'givers' instead of the biggest 'getters' (takers)." "Picking up the glove ... Microsoft's online magazine *Slate* took up that challenge launching the *Slate* 60, a list of the largest charitable donations in the country by families or individuals gathered from publicly available sources."

If this list becomes as important to the rich as the *Forbes* list has thus far been, it may well open up a veritable floodgate of financial help where it is needed most – in assisting the unemployed back to work and to self-esteem. For under Spiritual Law the wealthy have a duty to provide, not hand-outs, but means, schemes and employment, whereby the less fortunate can contribute meaningfully toward their respective societies, and to their own self-worth. Some of the super-wealthy are now doing more than that; by targeting the sick and disadvantaged.

A welcome new ethos among some of the super-wealthy has now seen many millions of dollars channelled toward projects such as medical aid to Africa. The work of the "Gates Foundation" founded, of course, by Bill and Melinda Gates, seems to have pricked the conscience of other wealthy individuals who are also now offering financial help to the needy.

Notwithstanding such generosity we should, nonetheless, not leave this particular segment without offering this most wonderfully appropriate Biblical quote:

> *"For what will it profit a man if he should gain the whole world and forfeit his life? "(lose his soul?)*
>
> (Mark 8:36, Fenton. Parenthetic addition mine.)

A quote from "Building Future Societies. Spiritual Principles of Nation Building", Chapter 2, p 39, Stephen Lampe, Millennium Press, offers a further reflective note:

> More than 150 years ago, a French economist, Pierre Boisguilbert came to the recognition of the utmost importance of balance. He wrote:
> "Only equilibrium (balance) can save everyone; and nature alone, to repeat, can achieve this. On our part, we should give and give, and nature will restore balance."

The right balance must be struck in all aspects of our lives and not just economic re-structuring. The rapid increase in one-parent families shows the urgent need to restore balance in personal relationships, in social interaction with others, and in all human activities. The breakdown of large nations to smaller ethnic states is nothing more than the restoration of balance to peoples once forced to become, for them, part of a larger and often alien system.

The British Commonwealth is one example of this ongoing process. Once an empire of disparate countries and peoples ruled by the force of arms of the "mother country", it has now developed into a *relatively* easy voluntary association of most of those former colonies, bonded by more or less common goals, aspirations and ideals. Such links, moreover, have allowed the many varied races in the Commonwealth to develop a generally greater degree of knowledge and tolerance toward each other, particularly in the areas of race and religion, than might otherwise have been the case under continued British military dominance. And that is as it should be.

In its current format, the British Commonwealth, *thus far*, stands as a reasonably good example of what can be achieved through voluntary goodwill, with the concomitant ability to play a beneficial role in international affairs. However, if the common binding force were the knowledge and application of The Spiritual Laws of Creation, the Commonwealth example and its resultant international effect would be much more powerful.

The Law of Balance between Giving and Taking may, if there is sufficient time left, one day play a fundamental part in true international understanding when peoples and races finally stand **SIDE BY SIDE**, helping and furthering one another in mutual respect. The ideal time for such a process to begin is always in the present of course. The vital recognition that every people, every race, possesses earthly and spiritual values which are indispensable for humanity as a whole will, hopefully, one day arrive. And because other peoples and races may not inherently possess exactly the same attributes, a vital exchange of those values should then become the norm. But such exchanges that occur must reflect the right balance in accordance with the outworking of this Law between Giving and Taking.

Whilst the inherent characteristics of The Law of Balance can obviously be applied to most situations, the most critical should be to urgently seek the correct balance between the ***material and spiritual*** in our individual lives. In the intellectual sense man presently stands astride the apex of his technological pyramid. Spiritually, though, he grovels in the dust at the base, stunted and blind. If any kind of reminders were needed to induce us to begin to redress the balance of the scales toward the spiritual, one need only look at everyday world events. In that clear revelation *humankind unequivocally reveals the level **it has chosen**!*

0.7 The Law of Rebirth!

0.7.1 Rebirth! – Fact or Fiction?

The one absolute we all accept without question, irrespective of race, religious beliefs or political leanings etc., is the factual reality of birth, life and death. These three facets, at least in their physical happening, also represent the only belief or reality for many. The processes of all three, moreover, are absolutely identical for all individuals insofar as the *mechanics* are concerned. Only the individual life paths will be different due to the factors of race, geographical location, education, wealth and status etc., but both the *spiritual and physical* **processes** *for each remain the same.*

The term "miracle of birth" reflects our amazement and wonder at this event. The Spiritual Laws that govern the development of the growing individual and determines the final characteristics of it are constant and unchangeable. Thus the many billions of human births have followed the same lawful process. Inherent in The Laws is certainly the provision for development, but not for wrong experimentation, deviation or transgression, however. So even when using the procedure of in-vitro fertilisation, doctors are not able to operate outside the parameters dictated by this universal Law.

It is the same with the death process. Without exception we are forced to accept the absolute inevitability of it at some point in life. Universal Laws operate here in their immovable perfection too. For the step from a living, breathing, animated physical body to a cold, lifeless shell is exactly the same everywhere in the world. The manner of dying may be vastly different, i.e., disease, war, illness, accident – in peaceful sleep even – but the process is nevertheless identical. Indeed, it could not be otherwise. Yet whilst we are able to observe the physical processes of the steps of birth and death, and can clearly see the after effects of birth, we do not necessarily accept that there may be after effects of earthly death too.

Why not, however? If the evidence of our own eyes with regard to the irrefutable processes of birth and death governed by strict, consistent laws in the *physical* happening can be readily accepted, why should it not be a simple step to know *intuitively* that the outworking of The Spiritual Laws do not simply come to a convenient halt at that point simply because we may believe or wish otherwise.

By virtue of the inviolability of those Laws, humankind can do little else but submit to them, for there is no other choice.

Even in cases of suicide or murder the physical processes must still inevitably be the same. However, even though The Laws are physical in their visible effect, they are, nevertheless, still Spiritual in origin. It is worth deep consideration that even the Son of God, Jesus, had to be born of a woman on earth. The Creator could not just simply place Him on the earth as a fully-grown man – notwithstanding the strong religious belief among many that: "God can do anything He pleases".

From that standpoint consider, again, the later words of Jesus:

> "*Do not imagine that I have come to abolish the law and the prophets; I have not come to abolish, but to complete them. For I tell you indeed, that until the heavens and the earth shall pass away, a single dot or hairstroke shall not disappear from the law, until all has been completed.*"
>
> (Matthew 5:17-18, Fenton.)

Thus, the "Natural Laws" could not be circumvented then, not even by Jesus Himself, nor can they be today – or ever. Not by force of arms, wealth, political power, scientific disbelief, rationalist theories and, not least, by religious dogma. Ultimately there is no choice for humankind but to submit to the processes outlined, since it is Spiritual Law that drives everything in Creation. By virtue of our free will we *can* choose to *oppose* those Laws. However, the outworking of them will eventually guarantee the appropriate kind of hard and bitter reaping for such opposition.

What we cannot change at all is the *actual* and lawful outworking of the death process itself. Since every incident or event that occurs must have some kind of starting point or origin, it should be a simple matter to deduce that the sudden, unexpected arrival of painful experiences in our lives can only be the result of a previous decision made elsewhere. *We constantly stand, therefore, in the centre of all our **returns**, both good and bad, exactly in accordance with all the free-will decisions responsible for **every returning reciprocal effect**.*

However, because there may be no recollection of the actual originating decision or event in the present lifetime of an affected individual, or in the lives of others closely associated with that person which could have brought about such a consequence, any such end-effect clearly presupposes another possibility, i.e., the concept of more than one earth life from where such an outcome could originate. As previously stated, this is not a view readily accepted in Western thinking, though it is a basic tenet of billions of the World's peoples. So just as we can reduce the question of whether there is life after death to either there is, or there is not – for it surely cannot be both – we can also ask the same of *one life versus many*.

Current Western thought in the scientific and intellectual disciplines, and/or in religious doctrines, offer few genuine solutions to society's increasing problems within the restrictive parameters of "the one-life concept". Unfortunately, therefore, disbelief or ignorance of The Law of Rebirth cannot, in any way, alter the truth of its actual reality and outworking. This widespread "unbelief of the West" *can* be accepted if there is nothing more than a purely physical body to contend with. Conversely, if the body *is* no more than just the physical shell – the cloak housing the actual you and me – then, just as the processes of the Law allow for **one** birth, why could it not allow for **others** where another, but different, "overcoat" is simply taken on in accordance with such Laws?

This particular insight provides the actual meaning about the promise of "the resurrection of the flesh", stated by Jesus. This "resurrection" does **not** mean that bodies long dead will suddenly rise out of their graves at some point soon and become clothed in the flesh of the original owner. This strange and totally illogical belief seemingly derives from the Scripture that ostensibly states that: "All *the* dead shall awaken." However, in the light of the rapidly increasing degeneration of all aspects of global human activity, if we exercise logic and reason to strive to determine what it might truly mean, then we will intuitively recognise that it is actually a *warning*. It is a warning, moreover, that lives the essence of The Law of Reciprocal Action, and is thus a severe warning to humankind to **spiritually** awaken.

Therefore, the true meaning is:

> "All **that** is dead shall be awakened." Thus it is the awakening of *all, everything*, that is **spiritually** dead.

The *alarming increase* in our problems globally can be more readily understood through that vital revelation. So all belief systems, all disciplines of human endeavour, everything that we have held sacrosanct or sacred, everything that we might thus far have stated to be inviolable; all must now be forced to show where it truly stands in relation to The Spiritual Laws of Creation. Thus the spiritual pressure that is now being exerted more powerfully with each passing day upon *all* our beliefs and activities, *forces the awakening* of those belief systems and activities. It does not matter whether they *ostensibly* hold scientific, philosophical, religious or political "truths". Without exception, *everything* will be subject to this severe and relentless cleansing and clarifying process.

All that does not stand true – thereby suffering collapse in the *awakening process* – thus reveals that it **was** dead and *needed* to be **awakened** i.e., *that it did not have as its foundation and guiding principle,* **the knowledge of The Spiritual Laws**. This "awakening process", this *resurrection,* applied in accordance with the inviolability of The Law of Rebirth, thus permits each one the opportunity to "put right" past wrongs. Through this mechanism of Divine Grace, man is gifted the means whereby he may *earn* his ascent [return] to his Spiritual origins, his true home. "Resurrection of the flesh" is thus a Divine Grace providing the means whereby we are given numerous opportunities to return to the earth to atone for past transgressions committed in the earthly.

Yet, despite inherently possessing clear and ultimately irrefutable logic, reincarnation as a concept has fuelled debate for centuries. Even though a very large proportion of the world's peoples accept it as a factual part of man's *total* existence, the Judaeo-Christian religions generally do not. The basic belief of reincarnation in some form or another has been accepted by most in the Indian sub-continent for the past 2,500 odd years, and in other parts of the world for a long time too. It is interesting to note, however, that the so decisively important doctrine of reincarnation – of rebirth as a human being – was only expunged from Christian creeds by a very small majority decision at the Council of Constantinople in 553 AD. What was effectively lost through that decision of appalling ignorance and ego was the greater understanding of the *seeming* inequality of the world and, indeed, the Love and Justice contained in The Creative Will of God.

Consider, if at that fateful Council meeting only a few men had decided differently, *reincarnation would now be a matter of course for Western "religions" also.* Had that happened, there would not exist the present fortress of doubt and prejudice against the whole notion of "rebirth". In its place would be greater freedom of thinking rather than this terribly unfortunate constraint into which our current thought-processes have fallen, and solely because of that unfortunate decision taken by a few powerful men centuries ago. In general, it has succeeded in removing any possible larger outlook to the greater connections of our existence, and to the incredible vastness of Creation as a whole.

Because of that decision, we have created the unhealthy situation of not readily accepting death as a natural part of life, or as an ongoing transitional step in our complete existence.[19]

The great difficulty with trying to meaningfully grapple with the rapidly increasing problems in society as a whole, is that there often *appears* to be no logical cause for it all. Is it any wonder that suicides are on the increase, particularly among the more impressionable young who are often too emotionally immature to cope with the *seemingly* insurmountable. They seek answers but no one will give them the only correct one. Our so-called "educators" reject the very thing that would provide the necessary enlightenment. Yet even *they* continue to ask – 'Why'? Australian Children's Advocate and "National Treasure", Professor Fiona Stanley, on the subject of increasing youth suicide there, soberly observed: "Despite all that we now know, and all the research that's been done, **nothing is getting any better**."

The concept of reincarnation will need to be accepted as fact if society wishes to find answers to its problems, for the deliberate rejection of it only pushes away the day of reckoning. It must be understood, however, that reincarnation is governed by the strictness of The Spiritual Laws too. Contrary to some beliefs and misconceptions, therefore, one **cannot** return as a tree, an insect, or an animal.

So, in direct contrast to the cultural or ethnic beliefs of various peoples, our ancestors cannot be such things as those. Inanimate objects have no connection with human spiritual origins, and neither do psychically produced forms that some indigenous groups revere. Therefore, living, animate creatures such as eagles, tigers and whales etc., must forever remain their own kind. Humankind's collective Spiritual ancestry can *only* centre around being human.

Simply and logically put, The Laws of Nature absolutely decree that we **cannot change our species**. They thus further decree that under The Law of Rebirth we can only return as human beings. Carrying with us, moreover, all that we have **previously sown**. Some experiences we are forced to live through may well have their origin in previous earth-lives. How we live our life now will determine what will come our way in the future, perhaps even in a later earth-life. Whole nations and races must collectively reap what they have sown as well.

The destruction of the Axis Powers during The Second World

---

[19] The details of that meeting are examined more specifically in specific Chapters in the Parent Book that outline the actual death process.

War is a particularly good example of whole peoples and races suffering collectively through the outworking of decisive Spiritual Laws in concert with their *free-will decision* to embark upon global war and conquest. And in the maelstrom of that conflict may be seen horrific outcomes for certain races; outcomes ultimately derived from decisions made in the long-distant past, but which required resolution in another place and time among other peoples. Under the aegis of The Laws of "Reciprocal Action", "Attraction..." and "Rebirth" mainly, the perfection of those Spiritual Laws decree that **events** which produce "mass victims of tyranny" do not necessarily have their **actual genesis** in the historical circumstances **immediately preceding** the particular incident or event.

The greater the extent and degree of suffering of a people or group, the longer the period of time required for the correct and lawful circumstances to bring about the reciprocal effect **to awaken that group to the reason for its suffering**. Ordinarily, the group or race imposing the suffering would then set in train the reciprocal consequences of its actions which it must expect to receive one day too. The difference now, however, is that the time of return is considerably shortened whereby all past events strive for resolution under the pressure of The Spiritual Laws as they drive the release of all reciprocity.

The Western medical profession's general refusal to accept this quite logical view of a multi-life concept and become locked, instead, into a single one unfortunately translates into the practice of often attempting to go beyond reasonable limits in order to preserve "life". At all costs seems to be the view, rather than simply accepting the dignified inevitably and reality of a "natural transition" to earthly death. Of course life should be extended for as long as it is reasonably possible to do so, but not at the expense of unnecessarily prolonging what should be regarded as the completely normal process of exiting earth-life. Neither should death be *desperately fought against* when medical reality clearly indicates an imminent demise. The dying one is not actually helped thereby.

Reincarnation offers the only viable mechanism for mankind to make rational sense of the misery, the suffering and the tragedies that beset the world today in such a relentless manner. Whilst it also brings good fortune and happiness for some, it is the tragedies that need more urgent clarification.[20] However, as the actuality of

---

[20]It is not the purpose of this Booklet to deal with this subject to any great degree, for it is more thoroughly examined and clarified in a particular Chapter in the Parent Work; to help clarify another contentious religious issue – that

reincarnation is a "Living Law of God" – which no one can change – it behoves us all to learn what we can about the actual mechanism and process which, in its concept and outworking, actually provides the greatest measure of certainty about earth-life and life thereafter.

The Indian sage Paramahansa Yogananda wrote much about how to live correctly. Perfectly correct living, however, is really only possible with the knowledge of all The Laws of Creation. Even though actively seeking what he intuitively perceived was that complete knowledge existing somewhere on earth during his lifetime, certain preconceptions he harboured effectively prevented his taking the final step to personal recognition when given the crucial opportunity which would have led him to it. Notwithstanding that missed vital moment, his inherent wisdom nevertheless offers a good blueprint for basically correct living. His knowledge of reincarnation offers a brief insight into his truthful wisdom.

From the sub-heading, **"How We Live This Life Determines What We Are in the Next."**:

> "We have been given the power to reason out where we go and whence we have come. But we don't take enough pains to analyse ourselves and our lives. Otherwise our common sense would tell us that whatever our character is today it will continue to be after death – perhaps a little better or a little worse, depending on how much effort we are making to improve ourselves. You go along 365 days a year, year after year, and perhaps you have made some progress, but your nature will be the same after death as it was before death. You will not become an angel just because you die! Only the body changes. Death makes no difference, otherwise. Death is like a gate you will pass through. Your body will be gone but you will be in every other respect the same. If you have a violent temper, you will not leave it behind, at death, with your physical body. Your violent temper will remain with you until you conquer it. If in your present life you have observed the laws of healthful living, in your next incarnation you will possess a healthy body. The last portion of life is more important than the first, because what you are at the end of this life is what you will be at the beginning of the next.
>
> The first part of life is usually stupidly misspent, in a sort of bewildered state. Then romance comes, and finally

---

of the "Second Death".

disease and old age; the struggle with the body starts... The body is a trouble most of the time:... Always trouble, trouble! *That is why it is so necessary to your happiness that you realize you are not the body...*"[21]

(Man's Eternal Quest, p 219. Italics mine.)

As a final notation on this subject, reincarnation, as an inviolable Spiritual Law, must live the fullness of that fact without deviation. This Law also naturally exists within The Laws of Nature, which themselves are a reflection of the Eternal Laws. All dovetail into each other in perfect outworking. As previously stated, perhaps the refusal of many Westerners to accept reincarnation may be due in part to the promoted belief of some Eastern religions that one may be required to return to the earth – for various purposes of atonement – as an animal, a bird or an insect even.

Atonement is a most necessary requirement in the outworking of our inherent free-will decision-making ability under The Law of Reciprocal Action – a Law which unequivocally states;

"...what a man sows, that he will also reap."

(Galatians 6:7, Fenton)

Reincarnation therefore provides the only "earthly" *long-term mechanism* under which this spiritually ordained atonement **can** be expiated. As it is also a Law of Nature or a natural Law, we strongly reiterate that such Laws unequivocally state that it is not possible to change one's species, *irrespective of any belief to the contrary.*

The inner animating core of man – his actual life-force – is **spirit,** whilst that of the animal is **soul.** They are two very different species of animating power from two different levels in Creation. Therefore, in this context, the human spirit must always remain a human spirit, with absolutely *no possibility* that it could somehow transmigrate across *immovable spiritual boundaries* to become a life-form **different** to that ordained for it by the unalterable Laws of Creation. So humans remain humans, **they cannot become animals**. And, just as surely:
Animals cannot "develop" into humans!

In summary the process of reincarnation, whereby a human spirit is ordained by Law to accept rebirth on earth, is subject to,

---

[21] An apt description from the Bible refers to the body as "the deadly carcass".

and affected by, the collective outworking of all The Spiritual Laws of Creation. The free-will decisions of his previous life, or lives, will determine who he will be in the next one, what his spiritual lessons will be, and what he can also spiritually offer that group of souls into which he will be incarnated – to those who will be his earthly family. That, in turn, will determine such factors as to whether he will be born handicapped or complete, whether his new circumstances will be one of wealth or struggle, whether of the same race, geographical location or religion as his last incarnation, or one completely different.

Irrespective of those considerations, however, the circumstances of his next incarnation will precisely offer the necessary conditions he will need for his further spiritual maturing. The key point in all of this is the fact that he is still master of his own destiny. In that sense his inherent spiritual free-will provides the mechanism whereby he can always and at any time set in place new decisions for himself. The new direction, called forth by those decisions, will of course change or modify his present life-path originally ordained for him by Law through the outworking of all his previous decisions. Certain *"experiences of the spirit"*, however, will be part of his necessary path and may perhaps even provide a lifetime of hard struggle.

Whether or not that is the case may well depend upon the lawful outcomes of previous personal decisions acting upon him as he lives out his present life. Even if he should live spiritually-correctly, yet experience a lifetime of struggle, The Spiritual Laws will still set in train beneficial returns for a future time. For the more *powerful experiences* will be impressed upon his spirit *in any case*, be it through *great joy* **or** *tragedy*.

Thus, The Laws of Creation intermesh to bring about precisely lawful outcomes. Yet it always remains with the individual as to what those personal outcomes will be. As stated regularly throughout the Parent Book, only the **decision** is **free**, the **consequences** are **not!** Thus, in cases where two options are presented, whilst we will always have a **50%** option or **choice**, there is always only a **100% outcome** <u>after</u> the decision has been taken. Of course there is nothing to prevent one from modifying or radically changing the original decision with a second, or even third one. Those decisional changes, of course, will ultimately be reflected in its corresponding outcome at some future point.

0.8 Grace! – A Gift of Divine Love.

Even though not perhaps a Law in the strictest sense, the inclusion of the key aspect of Grace in this Booklet about The Spiritual Laws is vital because the concept and outworking of the spiritual attribute of Grace impacts decisively and beneficially on the fate of anyone who recognises the error of their ways and subsequently seeks a more enlightened path. The entry of Grace into one's life, therefore, will manifest through the outworking of Spiritual Law in reciprocity deriving from spiritually-correct decision-making – even if the particular decision required needed to be a material one.

Grace is an inherent quality of Divine Love. Also inherent in Divine Love is Justice. However, the Love that is defined here has no affinity whatever with humankind's emotionally-distorted idea of this most noble Power. Thus, under the outworking of Grace – which *originates* from The Divine – help and guidance are given to humankind with each passing moment. In order to reap the benefits, however, the guidance needs first to be *recognised*, and then *lived* accordingly.

Since The Spiritual Laws contain both the cornerstones of Love and Justice, they return only what is *spiritually* beneficial. By heeding Spiritual Law, we give no cause for any such "unwanted returns". In its distilled essence, therefore, "Spiritual Love" is pure, even *severe* if necessary. In certain cases it *needs* to be *severe* in order to bring about the necessary *awakening* to force the question **"*why*"**! Yet we must ever be mindful of the fact that we ourselves will have given cause for that event or trial somewhere, sometime, in accordance with the inviolable outworking of The Spiritual Laws.

Thus the kind of Love outlined here is not the caricature spawned and given form by collective humankind, and which has become so distorted that it is now used to encompass virtually every kind of debased activity under "modern", liberal thinking. This human distortion carries no justice within it. In keeping with current, prevalent attitudes, attempts are continually made to separate that which cannot be separated – genuine Spiritual Love from true Spiritual Justice.

In the most wonderful of ironies, the twin forces of Spiritual Love and Justice will eventually teach humankind that they are, indeed, inseparable. We have produced a weak form we call love but which, in reality, is more often than not a mask and poor excuse for overly liberal, over-emotional and vacillating *self-indulgence*. In short, we have substituted the pure Power of Love with earthly emotionalism. In its pure form genuine Love stands far above such incorrect ideas. Compassion should not be confused with what is described here either, for compassion is an attribute of unconditional Love. When one has accepted, understood and finally worked through all that must be personally expiated, The Spiritual Laws or Rules then become strong and furthering helps for one's spiritual growth, thus expressing the Power of the genuine Love. The **"Gift of Grace"** lives in the essence of that inviolable Truth!

The **"Gift of Grace"** therefore permits even the worst transgressions to be completely expiated, if one *genuinely* seeks to put right his wrongs. Despite the fact that The Spiritual Laws operate strictly here, too, the overriding attribute contained within the outworking of The Laws in this case is that of Grace and forgiveness. If being "pursued by one's works" presupposes a "return" of even severe difficulty and hardship, it is important to understand that by simply *changing* our spiritual volition for the better, we automatically begin the process of *altering* the forms – both their intensity and severity – of "our wrong works" previously produced. For they will, at some future point, surely and certainly return to us.

Therefore, under the process of reciprocity in "awaiting our works", someone who has lived a life of dark, horrific deeds is absolutely condemned to fully reap his "personal whirlwind" either here on the earth or when passed from it, *so long as there is no effort or attempt to change his ways*. Total ignorance of this cause, or even disbelief of it, cannot alter the returning effects either. As we need to restate, this lawful path reflects Divine Justice that, at the same time, is also Divine Love.

Therefore, the returning reciprocal effect to a hardened soul should thus provide the necessary experiences and potential for a spiritual awakening, a re-appraisal of one's personal situation, and some deep "soul-searching". Should that individual stubbornly fight against this process, ***more of the same is assured***. Yet this should not be seen as some kind of retributive punishment from some arbitrary God or Power. It is simply the "personal reaping" from the *personal* "sowing", ***irrespective of when sown or why***.

What of one with many years of living a depraved or evil lifestyle, and with total and selfish disregard for the welfare of his victims, however? What happens when such a one suddenly finds oneself faced with the unnerving reality that his attitude and conduct were "all wrong"? What then? Ordinarily, we would probably say he still deserves to pay for everything he inflicted on others. According to societal Law, that would probably be the case and society would no doubt be well pleased with such an outcome. Indeed, it is appropriate that correct punishment be meted out, for society has a right to protection from such individuals. In any case, our earthly Laws should reflect the clear recognition that we cannot function without order.

Therefore, even if a "criminal" has been dealt with by the justice of the earthly courts, this does not mean that all is necessarily "paid for". The more crucial debt, **the spiritual**, may still await resolution. However, if our miscreant – through the honest recognition that his previous ways were wrong – then genuinely seeks to mend them and make atonement, he sets in place for himself the mechanism whereby the impact of the returning retroactive consequences of his previously dark volition can be greatly lessened. Of course the desire to want to change must be an absolutely genuine one, for The Spiritual Laws are not fooled by the subterfuge and deviousness that human beings often engage in. Genuine humility, moreover, must be an accompanying factor in such a change.

What, then, is that process? Because we possess the inherent attribute of "free will", and because there is only **one** *neutral power* streaming through and animating all of Creation including the material worlds, our "free-will" endowment ensures that this *neutral power* is *refracted through us* to good or evil purpose, **according to how we choose to use it.** Under the outworking of The Law of Attraction of Similar Species, if our volition is dark, we automatically make connections to, and attract in and surround ourselves with, similar species. If the opposite is the case, via the same process of connection and attraction, we lock ourselves into a vastly different kind of "power stream". It is one one that brings beneficial effects.

Thus, in the voluntary spiritual change that the felon of our example has undertaken, he has changed his "nature of attraction" from one originally leaning toward dark things to those much lighter. Since this change is subject to The Law of Spiritual Gravity also, there occurs within and around him a lightening effect as a result of his decision to change his ways for the good. Now he attracts to himself beneficial "forms" corresponding to his new volition. But where does this place him with regard to the returning effects of perhaps a long life of degrading deeds? The Law of Sowing and Reaping must still hold sway. That cannot change.

Now, however, through his newly-activated, lighter connections corresponding to the new volition with which he now surrounds himself – quite automatically – a lighter and stronger force envelops him. This acts like a cocoon against which some of the retroactive effects of his past volition can be deflected. Some may still penetrate to him. In which case they will be of such a nature as he still requires for growth and ascent and, moreover, may therefore need to be fully experienced materially for complete expiation under Spiritual Law.

The experiences from it, however, will enable him to further develop spiritually. Some returning effects may only need to be redeemed symbolically, perhaps something even as innocuous as a kind word to a complete stranger. Each case will be different for every individual but it will be in strict and inflexible accordance with Spiritual Law operating in concert with the Gift of Grace, so demonstrating both Perfect Justice and Perfect Love, two important cornerstones of The Spiritual Laws of Creation.

Therefore, if we do not wish to be pursued by any former "unpleasant works", it is essential that the knowledge of the Eternal Laws be regarded as a serious spur to help nullify the reciprocal effects of them. Thus, via the perfection of The Laws, we are enjoined to strive only for what is good. Such striving will ensure the reciprocal effect of greater peace and happiness under the "Gift" of Divine Grace!

Conclusion.

"Power comes out of the barrel of a gun!"

(Mao Tse Tung.)

"Physical strength will never permanently withstand the impact of spiritual force!"

(Franklin D. Roosevelt.)

"The pen is mightier than the sword!"

(From the original, "Arms give way to Persuasion." – Cicero.)

Here we have three vastly different quotes occupying opposite ends of the "spiritual spectrum". Each one, however, generating its own specific kind of "return" under the aegis of The Spiritual Laws. The first concerned solely with earthly results, but ultimately returning spiritually-driven corresponding ramifications of no small import, and the other two having connections to both.

In the first quote are sown the seeds of its own destruction because its inferior "form" is correspondingly attached to weaker and therefore lower and baser levels. The latter, however, if writing *Spiritual Truth*, is equal to the second because of its powerful connection to the source of all Life. By virtue of that fact, any such writings connected to that source produce "forms of spiritual power", as opposed to the "baser forms" produced by the gun *if* the use of it is for strictly totalitarian purposes with the aim being control and/or enslavement.

Whilst The Spiritual Laws are the infallible and unalterable *driving mechanism* which produce the consequence or outcome for every decision made, it is vital to understand that any spiritual transgression incurred will be made more against the "rules for correct living". They are those that all the great religions and spiritual and philosophic teachings have recognised and espoused over millennia. Thus one *can* transgress The Law of Balance. In the true sense of the word, however, one cannot actually *transgress* The Laws of "Rebirth", "Attraction... " or "Spiritual Gravity" etc.. However, transgressions against the "rules of life" such as are stated in The Ten Commandments, for example, even if done in complete ignorance of them, nevertheless unequivocally sets in motion the driving **return** mechanism that is inherent in the *power* of Spiritual Law. In this case, more specifically in The Law of Reciprocal Action (Sowing and Reaping.)

The reader should thus understand that The Ten Commandments, which the Law-Giver Moses received for **all** of humankind, are the necessary accompaniment of **The Spiritual Laws of Creation**. Both issue from the hand of **The Creator** for the harmonious order of **His Creation**. However, whilst they are "The Rules", so to speak, The Laws that drive and sustain everything are vitally important to know so that we may understand *why* **The Ten Commandments** must be regarded as very necessary "Rules for correct living".

It is equally important to recognise, also, that it is *Spiritual Power* that we actually use in all decision-making. Even our thought processes utilise the same power. It permeates every part of Creation, for that is the life force of the whole. However, it does not at all mean that our utilisation of that power necessarily produces genuinely spiritual outcomes. Unfortunately, and as global societies clearly reveal, the volition of humankind has produced mainly aspiritual ones. Clearly evidenced by the global situation, the mechanism inherent in The Spiritual Laws drives everything to its particular outcome.

0.8.1 A Brief Illustration of Why Recognition of The Law is a "Crucial Imperative" for all of humanity right now.

The inviolable outworking of The Law of Attraction of Similar Species coupled with the severe admonition: "...by their works ye shall know them", can be seen very, very clearly now in the worsening state of virtually all global societies and in our rapidly degrading environment. Thousands upon thousands of years of "producing works" absolutely opposed to The Laws of Life have brought us to a point of *final crisis*. If we have learned little else in our long tenure on earth on which we humans were tasked to be the guardians and nurturers of truth and law and protector of the bounty which the earth provided, we will certainly now learn that The Law is absolute and it is inviolable. We will experience more and more severely the foolishness of our collective transgressions.

The **"Crucial Imperative"** for global humanity now is to recognise the truth of **The One Law** for all of humankind. The many long centuries where religion and not truth held sway to produce so much bloodshed and slaughter, has "heaped-up" an invisible yet very menacing "tsunami of reciprocity" which will break with *greater devastating force* over mankind *than is already occurring at present*. Earth-science and earth-business, co-instigators and co-producers of products and processes that have fashioned virtually all the poisons which contaminate land, water, people and animals alike; you, too, have added your terrible share. It will not be enough to say: *"But we produced good things too."*

The few good things produced and/or undertaken have never been sufficient to offset the development and growth of "power centres" exactly commensurate with the free-will production of "goods and services" that have no affinity with the True Laws of Creation, but were nevertheless produced by religious and scientific ignorance, ego and arrogance.

The aeons-long transgressions against Divine Law have, under the aegis of "The Law of Attraction of Similar Species" primarily, produced our vast, dark "power centres". Undetectable to the earthly senses and *disbelieving scientific empiricism*, the greater mass of each one quietly waits for the moment when precise outworking of The Law decrees its time of *full release* upon global humanity.

The knowledge of The Spiritual Laws permits us the correct understanding of our overall purpose in life. The degree to which those Laws have been explored should be sufficient for at least a basic understanding of our "reason for being". Only with the help of the knowledge of them could this Booklet ever be offered.

0.9 Postscript.

The Parent Work, from which this Booklet is substantially derived, also includes a Chapter on our Origins, (a sister Booklet as well) for it is vital to recognise and understand that crucial aspect too. Whilst The Spiritual Laws are very necessary for understanding *what* our free will decision-making process will return to us in the *how* and the *why* of the overall process, that knowledge cannot stand completely alone.

We also require the further recognition of our Spiritual, and therefore actual, origins – our "whither and why". For to that home we can return provided we have made the correct decisions throughout life to achieve that desirable outcome. Irrespective of whether made consciously or unconsciously, however, they are choices nevertheless driven by, or taken under, the aegis of:

The Spiritual Laws of Creation:

CREATION-LAW!

Bibliography.

1. Key knowledge sourced from: *In the Light of Truth: The Grail Message by Abd-ru-shin*. 3 Vol. Edition. Published by Stiftung Gralsbotschaft, Stuttgart, Germany.

2. *Bible "Mysteries" Explained: Understanding "Global Societal Collapse" from The "SCIENCE" in The Bible; What Every Scientist, Bible Scholar and Ordinary Man Meeds to Know.* Charles S Brown. Crystal Publishing, 2011, New Zealand.

3. *The Gathering Apocalypse and World Judgement*, Charles S Brown. Crystal Publishing, 2005, New Zealand.

4. *The Holy Bible in Modern English*, Ferrar Fenton, Destiny Publishers, Massachusetts U.S.A. 1966 Edition.

5. *The Holy Bible, Authorised (King James) Version*, Eyre and Spottiswoode (Publishers) Ltd., Great Britain.

6. *The Jerusalem Bible, Reader's Edition*, First published 1968, Darton, Longman and Todd Ltd., London.

7. *The Christian and Reincarnation*, Stephen Lampe, Millenium Press (UK) 1990.

8. *Building Future Societies*, Stephen Lampe, Millenium Press (UK) 1994.

9. *The Concise Oxford Dictionary of Proverbs*, 1983 Edition, Oxford University Press, First Printing 1982, USA, New England Journal of Medicine.

10. *Ideas and Opinions*, Albert Einstein, Bonanza Books, New York, 1954.

11. *Philosophy History and Problems*, Third Edition, Samuel Enoch Stumpf, McGraw-Hill, USA 1983.

12. *The Nature Of The Gods*, Cicero, Penguin Classics, 1972 Edition, Translation by Horace C P Macgregor, Printed by Richard Clay (S E Asia) Pte. Ltd. Reprinted 1978, 1984.

13. *Sophie's World*, Jostein Gaardner, Phoenix House, Great Britain, 1996 Edition.

14. *Autobiography of a Yogi*, Paramahansa Yogananda, First published 1946, Random House.

15. *Man's Eternal Quest*, Paramahansa Yogananda, Collected Talks and Essays on Realizing God in Daily Life, Volume 1.

16. *The Helmet and the Cross* W. H. Canaway.Century Publishers. London 1986.

17. *Chief Seattle environmental address.* Friends' of the Earth

18. Dr. Alan Duggan. Researcher of Male Health. (Australia.)

19. Professor Fiona Stanley. Australian Children's Advocate and 'National Treasure'.

20. Kathleen Quinlivan. Researcher. (New Zealand.)

21. Rev. Gerald Hadlow. (New Zealand.)

0.10 The Parent Book:

<u>Formerly</u>:

"The Gathering Apocalypse and World Judgement; What It Brings – Even Now – And Why" [See Back Cover.]

Available in **New Zealand** at:
http://www.publishme.co.nz

Or at **www.crystalbooks.org**

<u>Now:</u>

BIBLE "MYSTERIES" EXPLAINED
[Revised Second Edition]
Understanding "Global Societal Collapse" from The "Science" in The Bible;
What Every Scientist, Bible Scholar and Ordinary Man Needs to Know!

> The **Revised Second Edition** of this book is more comprehensive in that it now explains How and Why the 2008 global economic collapse occurred, but also when the seeds that wrought the How and Why were sown, and by whom. [Chapter 3: **The Spiritual Laws: The Necessary Knowledge**
> 3.3.3 "Ten Men Will Take Counsel And It Will Come To Nought."
> 3.3.4 The Interlinked Global Monetary System "Reaping The Whirlwind." A Brief History Lesson.]

> Additional information about the events surrounding the last day of Jesus's life, from His arrest in the Garden of Gethsemane to His murder at Golgotha, is now included.
> The interesting question of the "Seven Churches in Asia-Minor" from The Book Of Revelation is examined more critically. Necessarily using the discoveries and mathematics of present-day cosmology, the revealing conclusion of the true meaning perfectly resonates with the intuitive perception of the great mathematician, astronomer, theologian and scientist, Sir Isaac Newton.

This book, the result of many years of inner seeking and empirical research, offers *serious* seekers of the Truth a comprehensive understanding of the origin, meaning and purpose of human life; material and spiritual.

Beginning with **The Crucial Imperatives: Nine key points** that *must* be taken into consideration if logical and reasoned answers to humankind's Whence, Whither and Why is *ever* to be understood; the book takes the reader step by step through an understanding of man's **Spiritual Origins, The Spiritual Laws of Creation**, the difference between **The First Death** and **The Second Death; Elemental Lore** [of Nature]; **Jesus! His Birth, Death and Resurrection** [a revisionist analysis]; before examining the truly 'mind-expanding' meaning of **"The 7 Churches in Asia"** from **The Book of Revelation**.

The key knowledge helps explain *why* there actually are **Two Sons of God**– final Chapter. It is key precisely because all other knowledge stems from that reality.

On reading the Work, the genuine seeker will clearly see that a conditioning process, set in place by religious authorities from the outset, over millennia has wrought appalling suffering through their inexcusable distortions of the Teachings of **The Truth** that once issued pristine and sublime from the Pure Holiness of its Bringer: **Jesus, The Son Of God!**

Now, because of those distortions, humankind is as a rudderless wreck on an increasingly stormy sea. Our many and increasing problems were not brought upon us by any kind of arbitrary randomness, but through *our constant and stubborn refusal to live according to the very Laws of Life which* **alone** *guarantee knowledge, peace and harmony.*

At the same time, however, – and precisely through the knowledge of those Laws – the way is shown in *how* we can *change* global societies *for the better*. Quite logically, if we continue down our present path for much longer *without such change*, the immutable outworking of **The Law** *will simply bring to an end* all that which *human thought and endeavour* had sought to establish and/or erect *in place of* the immutable and inviolable aegis of: **The One Law!**

CREATION-LAW!

The Parent Work explains the How, the What and the Why!

Available in:

N.Z.:http://www.publishme.co.nz

Or – **http://www.crystalbooks.org**

Table of Contents

DEDICATION
Foreword
Acknowledgements
Author's Note
Pope Benedict's Regensburg Address
Preface

1 The Crucial Imperatives

    1.1 Crucial Imperative no 1: "The Scientific Bible..."
    1.2 Crucial Imperative no 2: "The Duality of Man..."
    1.3 Crucial Imperative no 3: "The Spirit Within..."
    1.4 Crucial Imperative no 4: "The True Nature of The Forces of Nature..."
    1.5 Crucial Imperative no 5: "The Finite Universe..."
    1.6 Crucial Imperative no 6: "The Immutability of THE LAW..."
    1.7 Crucial Imperative no 7: "The Prophetic Bible..."
    1.8 Crucial Imperative no 8: "Why We Possess Free Will..."
    1.9 Crucial Imperative no 9: "The Interconnectedness of All Events..."

2 The Origins of Man –
"Genesis" and Science Agree

    2.1 The "First" Creation
    2.1 The "Subsequent" Creation for Earth-man
    2.1 The 'Real' Human/Chimp Split: The 'How' and The 'Why'
    2.2 Chronology of the Creation Process
      2.2.1 The Key Points

3 The Spiritual Laws –
The Necessary Knowledge

    3.1 The Nature of The Spiritual Principles
    3.2 The Law of Movement
    3.3 The Law of Reciprocal Action
      3.3.1 Faith Versus Works
      3.3.2 Attitude to the Suffering
    3.4 "Ten Men Will Take Counsel And It Will Come To Nought."
      3.4.1 The Interlinked Global Monetary System
      "Reaping The Whirlwind" A Brief History Lesson
    3.5 The Law of Attraction of Similar Species

3.5.1 Spiritual Qualities as the First Consideration
   3.5.2 Families and Children
   3.5.3 Why There is so much Violence and Evil on Earth:
   The "Divine Warning" to Mothers
   3.5.4 The Universal Pain of Childbirth:
   The Enlarging Baby Cranium: A Medical "Mystery"
   3.5.5 Sexual Orientation and Creation-Law
3.6 The Law of Spiritual Gravity!
3.7 The Law of Balance!
   3.7.1 To Give, or to Take?
3.8 The Law of Rebirth
3.9 Grace!: A Gift of Divine Love
3.10 Conclusion
   3.10.1 Recognition of The Law!:
The "Crucial Imperative" for all of humanity.

4 Elemental Lore Of Nature

4.1 The Circle of Life
4.2 Earth-science and Elemental Lore
4.3 Philosophic and Religious Connections to
Elemental Lore
   4.3.1 The Prophet Isaiah's "Reeling Earth"
4.4 Native American Spirituality: A European View
   4.4.1 Excerpts from Chief Seattle's Address
4.5 The Elemental Connection to the Animal Kingdom
4.6 The Elemental Connection to the Human World
   4.6.1 "Avatar": The 'Too-Late Lesson' for Global Humanity

5 JESUS: His Birth, Death and Resurrection

5.1 Introduction
5.2 JESUS: His Birth, Death and Resurrection
5.3 "Virgin" Birth and "Immaculate" Conception
5.4 Mission of the "Three Wise Men"
5.5 Resurrection and Ascension
5.6 Jewish Condemnation of The Son of God
5.7 The 'Revelation' and The Holy Grail
   5.7.1 The Eucharistic Motif
   5.7.2 The Grail Motif
5.8 Crucifixion of the Son of God:
Medical Forensics Speak
   5.8.1 The Roman 'Flagrum':
The 'Scourging' of "The Son Of God"
   5.8.2 The 'Burden' of the Cross
   5.9 The 'Murder' at Golgotha
   5.9.1 The 'Nailing'
   5.9.2 His Final Moments
   5.10 One Solitary Life

6 Stigmata

6.1 The Turin Shroud
6.2 Stigmatics
6.3 The Third Fatima Prophecy
6.4 Christendom's Bondage to 'Distortions' of Bible Truths

7 Right Bible/Wrong Bible

7.1 The Number 666 of The Revelation
7.2 Fenton's Crucial Insight to The Book of Genesis
7.3 Intellectual Volition versus Spiritual Volition
7.3.1 Intellectual Volition
7.3.2 Spiritual Volition
7.4 Summary of Key Points of the 'Creation' Process
7.5 Fentons Translation of The Bible

8 The Emergence of Language

8.1 The Development and Spiritual Ramification of: The "Forming" Word!
8.2 The Biblical "Fall of Man": A Disastrous Legacy for Global Humanity
8.2.1 The Enlarging Baby Cranium: The "Reason"
8.3 The Two "Faces" of Language: Spiritual and Non-Spiritual "Examples"
8.4 Language in American Culture and "Entertainment"

9 The First Death

9.1 "Death, the Great Leveller"
9.2 Jesus – "Calling the Dead to Life"
9.3 The Nature of Hell
9.4 The Ramifications of Loud Wailing
9.5 Death of a Soldier

10 The Second Death

10.1 One Life – or Many Lives?
10.2 Earthbound Souls
10.2.1 The Earthbound Soldier
10.3 Hypnotism – a Spiritual Crime
10.4 The Danger of Leading Astray
10.5 The "Second Death" Process

11 The "Seven Churches in Asia" – The Revelation

11.1 The Vision in Patmos
11.1.1 To the Assembly in Ephesus
11.2 Sir Isaac Newton's "Plan of The World"
11.2.1 The 'Mathematics' of Cosmology: The "Big Bang" and "Inflation" Model
11.2.2 The "Big Bang": A Problematic Theory Lost in The "Hubble Bubble"
11.3 The 'Revelation' of "The Plan of The World"
11.3.1 An Astronomy Lecturer's Recognition

12 THE TWO SONS OF GOD!

    12.1 Introduction
    12.2 THE TWO SONS OF GOD
    12.3 The Revelation of "The Other Son"
    12.4 The Disciples' Confusion
    12.5 "HE" Who Is "Enthroned"
    12.6 Destruction by "Fire"
    12.7 The Rapture
    12.8 THE PROCLAMATION

Epilogue
Bibliography

THE BOOKLET SERIES

* * * * *

THE TWO SONS OF GOD

The Son of Man and The Son of God
What The Bible Really Says

* * * * *

JESUS!:
His Birth, Death and Resurrection

A Revisionist Analysis of the "Sacrosanct" Christian Viewpoint

* * * * *

THE SPIRITUAL LAWS OF CREATION

The Crucial Knowledge for Humankind

* * * * *

WHITHER COMETH HUMANKIND?
(The Origins of Man) *Genesis and Science Agree*

* * * * *

THE "7 CHURCHES" Of THE "REVELATION"

What the "Hubble" Will Never See
Sir Isaac Newton's "Plan of The World"

* * * * *

www.ingramcontent.com/pod-product-compliance
Lightning Source LLC
Chambersburg PA
CBHW071507040426
42444CB00008B/1539